Apress Pocket Guides

Apress Pocket Guides present concise summaries of cutting-edge developments and working practices throughout the tech industry. Shorter in length, books in this series aims to deliver quick-to-read guides that are easy to absorb, perfect for the time-poor professional.

This series covers the full spectrum of topics relevant to the modern industry, from security, AI, machine learning, cloud computing, web development, product design, to programming techniques and business topics too.

Typical topics might include:

- A concise guide to a particular topic, method, function or framework
- Professional best practices and industry trends
- A snapshot of a hot or emerging topic
- Industry case studies
- Concise presentations of core concepts suited for students and those interested in entering the tech industry
- Short reference guides outlining 'need-to-know' concepts and practices.

More information about this series at `https://link.springer.com/bookseries/17385`.

Beginning Spring AI

A Quick Guide to AI Engineering in Spring

Andrew Lombardi
Joseph Ottinger

apress®

Beginning Spring AI: A Quick Guide to AI Engineering in Spring

Andrew Lombardi
Laguna Beach, CA, USA

Joseph Ottinger
Youngsville, NC, USA

ISBN-13 (pbk): 979-8-8688-1290-3 ISBN-13 (electronic): 979-8-8688-1291-0
https://doi.org/10.1007/979-8-8688-1291-0

Copyright © 2025 by Andrew Lombardi and Joseph Ottinger

This work is subject to copyright. All rights are reserved by the Publisher, whether the whole or part of the material is concerned, specifically the rights of translation, reprinting, reuse of illustrations, recitation, broadcasting, reproduction on microfilms or in any other physical way, and transmission or information storage and retrieval, electronic adaptation, computer software, or by similar or dissimilar methodology now known or hereafter developed.

Trademarked names, logos, and images may appear in this book. Rather than use a trademark symbol with every occurrence of a trademarked name, logo, or image we use the names, logos, and images only in an editorial fashion and to the benefit of the trademark owner, with no intention of infringement of the trademark.

The use in this publication of trade names, trademarks, service marks, and similar terms, even if they are not identified as such, is not to be taken as an expression of opinion as to whether or not they are subject to proprietary rights.

While the advice and information in this book are believed to be true and accurate at the date of publication, neither the authors nor the editors nor the publisher can accept any legal responsibility for any errors or omissions that may be made. The publisher makes no warranty, express or implied, with respect to the material contained herein.

Managing Director, Apress Media LLC: Welmoed Spahr
Acquisitions Editor: Melissa Duffy
Development Editor: Laura Berendson
Coordinating Editor: Gryffin Winkler

Cover designed by eStudioCalamar

Distributed to the book trade worldwide by Apress Media, LLC, 1 New York Plaza, New York, NY 10004, U.S.A. Phone 1-800-SPRINGER, fax (201) 348-4505, e-mail orders-ny@springer-sbm.com, or visit www.springeronline.com. Apress Media, LLC is a California LLC and the sole member (owner) is Springer Science + Business Media Finance Inc (SSBM Finance Inc). SSBM Finance Inc is a **Delaware** corporation.

For information on translations, please e-mail booktranslations@springernature.com; for reprint, paperback, or audio rights, please e-mail bookpermissions@springernature.com.

Apress titles may be purchased in bulk for academic, corporate, or promotional use. eBook versions and licenses are also available for most titles. For more information, reference our Print and eBook Bulk Sales web page at http://www.apress.com/bulk-sales.

Any source code or other supplementary material referenced by the author in this book is available to readers on GitHub (https://github.com/Apress). For more detailed information, please visit https://www.apress.com/gp/services/source-code.

If disposing of this product, please recycle the paper

*For my wife, my artistic love, and our kids:
the philosophers, adventurers, and creators who
make life an endless adventure.*

Table of Contents

About the Authors xi

About the Technical Reviewer xiii

Acknowledgments xv

Introduction xvii

Chapter 1: Introduction 1
    AI Is Everywhere 1
    What *Is* AI, Really? 3
    The Scope of This Book 6
    How Can AIs Be Used? 7
    How Do You Choose an AI? 8
    How Much Does It Actually Cost? 9
    What This Book Isn't 11
    Next Steps 12

Chapter 2: Getting Started 13
    The Project Structure 13
    Spring AI 22
        Getting the OpenAI Key 23
        Our First OpenAI Query 26

TABLE OF CONTENTS

Choosing a Different Model 33
Temperature 37
Conversations and Roles 48
Next Steps 55

Chapter 3: Asking Questions and Using Data 57

Interacting with an AI 57
Working with the "Real World" 59
Providing Access to Your Data 71
    Building the Callable for Spring AI 73
    Changing a Light 81
    Structured Output 87
Applying This in Your Code 93
Next Steps 93

Chapter 4: Working with Audio 95

Generating and Processing Audio 95
    The AI Spoken Word 96
    Transcription 107
    REST Example 113
    A Simple Voice Assistant 120
Next Steps 131

Chapter 5: Generating Images 133

Generating and Recognizing Images 133
    Image Generation 141
    Multimodality Recognition 147
    Lights, Camera, AI 153
Next Steps 157

Chapter 6: Navigating AI in Engineering 159
A Practical Exploration of AI-Aided Development 159
Dangers in Applying AI in Engineering 161
Legal and Ethical Issues 163
Data Visibility and Transparency 164
Effective Prompt Engineering 165
Next Steps 167

Index 169

About the Authors

Andrew Lombardi is a veteran entrepreneur and software engineer. He's been running the consulting firm Mystic Coders for 25 years, authored multiple outstanding books on Spring for Apress and WebSocket for O'Reilly, coding, speaking internationally, and offering technical guidance to companies as large as Airbus and companies as controversial and unique as Twitter 1.0. He firmly believes that the best thing he's done so far is being a great dad.

Joseph B. Ottinger is a distributed systems architect with experience in many cloud platforms. He was the editor-in-chief of both the *Java Developer Journal* and TheServerSide.com and has also contributed to many, many publications, open source projects, and commercial projects over the years, using many different languages (but primarily Java, Kotlin, Python, and JavaScript). He's also a previously published author online (with too many publications to note individually) and in print, through Apress.

About the Technical Reviewer

Manuel Jordan Elera is an autodidactic developer and researcher who enjoys learning new technologies for his own experiments and creating new integrations. Manuel won the Springy Award 2013 Community Champion and Spring Champion. In his little free time, he reads the Bible and composes music on his guitar. Manuel is known as dr_pompeii. He has tech-reviewed numerous books, including *Pro Spring MVC with WebFlux* (Apress, 2020), *Pro Spring Boot 2* (Apress, 2019), *Rapid Java Persistence and Microservices* (Apress, 2019), *Java Language Features* (Apress, 2018), *Spring Boot 2 Recipes* (Apress, 2018), and *Java APIs, Extensions and Libraries* (Apress, 2018). You can read his detailed tutorials on Spring technologies and contact him through his blog at www.manueljordanelera.blogspot.com. You can follow Manuel on his Twitter account, @dr_pompeii.

Acknowledgments

I would like to thank my family for supporting me during the writing of this book for the last few months along with crazy work running the company. I'd like to thank Joe for writing another book together which has turned out some pretty useful and interesting text as a team, our friends who remind me that there is also life outside of a screen and sunshine, rainbows, and the blinking cursor which is a prompt to keep going.

—Andrew Lombardi

I would like to thank whoever came up with the idea of thanking people in the front matter for books. Apparently, it's been done for pretty much the entire history of literature, originally used to credit deities and other patrons, so maybe we get to thank the purveyors of bad copper somehow.... This has not been a good acknowledgments paragraph, so let me try to rescue it somehow: I'd like to thank my family for their constant and undeserved encouragement, Andrew for putting up with my oddball ideas, the various small animals I keep throwing seeds to in my backyard for keeping me amused and appreciative, my wife, along with eden Hudson and Jess Astra for reminding me sometimes what a joy it is to read as well as write, and most of all, *you*, dear reader, for being willing to learn and grow with us. And spaghetti. I almost forgot to thank spaghetti.

—Joseph Ottinger

Introduction

Welcome to *Beginning Spring AI!*

Artificial intelligence has rapidly evolved over the last several years, and its influence now reaches into virtually every corner of modern software development. From generating text and images on-demand to analyzing audio content and extracting meaningful insights, AI is no longer the next frontier—it's a set of powerful tools ready to be applied right now. The Spring ecosystem, known for its robust and developer-friendly frameworks, has embraced this new era through Spring AI, a suite of libraries that serve as a gateway into the world of large language models (LLMs) and other advanced AI services.

What Is Spring AI?

Spring AI represents a cohesive set of abstractions and utilities that bridge your Spring-based applications with leading AI platforms. By simplifying complex integrations, Spring AI empowers you to connect to popular text, image, and audio models using a standardized approach—eliminating the need to learn multiple proprietary APIs or wrestle with inconsistent data formats. Instead, you can leverage a consistent, Spring-friendly programming model to interact with models like ChatGPT, stable diffusion image models, and speech-to-text engines, all within the familiar boundaries of your existing Spring projects.

INTRODUCTION

What You'll Learn in This Book

In this straightforward yet comprehensive guide, you will gain the practical knowledge and hands-on experience necessary to start building AI-enhanced applications right away. We begin by walking through project setup and configuration, ensuring you have a solid foundation for adding AI functionalities to your Spring-based environment.

1. **Connecting to ChatGPT and Other Large Language Models**
   Learn how to integrate large language models into your workflow. From the straightforward task of handling simple text queries, you'll progress toward generating structured content suitable for predictable, repeatable outputs. You'll also see how LLMs can be granted controlled access to your proprietary data, enabling sophisticated chatbots and assistants capable of interacting with real-world systems—from inventory databases to IoT devices—based on user input.

2. **Audio Generation and Analysis**
   Move beyond text-based content and tap into the world of audio. Discover how to instruct an LLM to create audio outputs—from synthetic speech to sonic branding elements—and then learn how to analyze spoken words. This capability opens up possibilities such as creating voice interfaces, automated transcription services, and real-time sentiment analysis for customer support calls.

3. **Visual Content Creation and Interpretation**
   Unleash the power of image-based AI models. You'll see how to use LLMs to generate entirely new images or enhance existing ones. On the flip side, you'll learn how to have an AI model interpret and describe visual content, making it possible for your applications to "see" and understand the world around them, from recognizing products in a catalog to summarizing complex diagrams for accessibility.

4. **Ethical, Legal, and Cost Considerations**
   While the potential of AI is vast, it's essential to understand its implications. We'll address common concerns around the ethical use of AI, highlight privacy and compliance considerations, and discuss cost management strategies. You'll gain the insights needed to responsibly build and deploy AI solutions that respect user data, operate transparently, and control expenses.

Why Spring AI?

By the end of this book, you'll have a toolkit that allows you to interact with multiple AI services through a single, coherent approach. Spring AI's abstraction layers and its deep integration with the broader Spring ecosystem significantly reduce the learning curve. You'll be able to plug into cutting-edge AI models using a codebase that is both approachable and maintainable—letting you focus on creating value instead of wrestling with technical minutiae.

INTRODUCTION

Your Journey Begins

As you turn the pages, you'll progress from foundational setup tasks to crafting sophisticated, AI-driven features. You'll discover not only how to leverage the capabilities of large language models but also how to integrate them seamlessly into real-world applications, from text-based assistants to voice-driven interfaces and vision-based analyzers.

Whether you're a seasoned Spring developer looking to add AI to your skill set, or you're new to the Spring ecosystem and want to start your journey at the cutting edge, this book is your guide to building smarter, more responsive, and more dynamic applications. Let's dive in and uncover the power of Spring AI together!

CHAPTER 1

Introduction

Welcome to *Beginning Spring AI*!

"Spring AI" refers to a suite of libraries within the Spring Framework designed to help programmers harness some of the most popular artificial intelligence (AI) technologies available today.

In this book, we'll take you on a guided tour of these libraries and their features. Our goal is not to provide a comprehensive reference on every feature but to offer enough information so you can see the potential of these technologies and use the majority of what you find most valuable.

> **Note** This chapter does not contain code. It lays a foundational understanding of AI, providing key definitions and concepts, as well as an overview of the technologies covered in this book. If you prefer diving right into the code, feel free to skip ahead to Chapter 2. However, we suggest revisiting this chapter later on, as it contains valuable insights that will enhance your understanding.

AI Is Everywhere

It's nearly impossible to browse the Internet today without encountering AI in some form. Whether it's a simple search for information, or summarizing content, possibly writing prompts on Quora, or creating

CHAPTER 1   INTRODUCTION

visual arts or music, AI is being applied across numerous domains. There are even entire songs generated by AI that some may find quite respectable.

For programmers, most IDEs now come with AI integrations, suggesting code completions and improvements. With the right prompts, it's possible to have an AI generate substantial portions of a working application, causing some managers to wonder if they even need human engineers anymore.[1]

Authors also feel the impact of AI "writing." Many tools now suggest grammar and spelling corrections, as well as more nuanced changes, to evoke a specific tone or style. AI can even write stories, and when given detailed prompts, the results can sometimes pass for human-written content.

Note   It's worth noting for the record: This book has indeed been impacted by AI, and we'll point out why and how later. We promise. At least, that's what the AI said to say. Or did it write it? Sometimes it's hard to tell.[2]

This raises an important question: Are humans being replaced by machines? If AI can create applications, music, or stories that rival human quality, then why do we need humans at all? There are several compelling answers to this, and some less convincing ones as well.

---

[1] Spoiler alert: Yes, the managers do need human engineers. We'll get to why soon, some in this chapter and some in Chapter 6.

[2] This is intended to be humor. If an AI generates any actual content of note in this book, we'll be pointing it out, even if it's not obvious. With that said, when we say AI is used in many writing tools, we mean it; a lot of our grammar was checked and occasionally fixed by AI. It's also worth noting that not even *one* of the footnotes was suggested by an AI—or, indeed, any human.

CHAPTER 1   INTRODUCTION

What *Is* AI, Really?

Let's start by clarifying what AI is. "Artificial intelligence" is a broad term with numerous applications, and we certainly won't cover all—or even most—of them in this book.

Here's how an AI (ChatGPT, using the GPT-4o model, specifically) summarized artificial intelligence:

```
Artificial Intelligence (AI) refers to the development
of computer systems that can perform tasks that normally
require human intelligence, such as learning, problem-solving,
and understanding language. At its core, AI uses mathematical
models to make decisions and predictions—ranging from
simpler approaches like Markov chains, which predict
sequences of events, to more complex systems like recommender
algorithms that suggest movies or products based on user
preferences. With advancements in AI, more sophisticated models
like Large Language Models (LLMs) have emerged, allowing
systems to understand and generate human-like text. These
models can be integrated into applications, such as those
built with Spring AI, to automate and enhance various
tasks across industries.
```

Not bad, ChatGPT! This example demonstrates a "good use" of AI: providing a *generally* concise and relevant summary on a topic. The prompt used here asked for a brief description of AI's evolution, focusing on widely adopted technologies like Large Language Models (LLMs), which we'll explore further in this book.

In the end, it's all literally math, as the paragraph suggested: an input is reduced to a series of numbers, and the AI ... does something with those numbers (what it does depends on the type of AI and its purpose). It then generates *more* numbers, and those numbers map to an output—and that applies to nearly every AI model, including the one that generated that paragraph.

3

CHAPTER 1   INTRODUCTION

Some of the earliest uses of AI models—early enough that some might scoff at the reference to them as "artificial intelligence"—were for tasks like weather prediction or making simple probabilistic decisions.

One simple modeling type is the Markov chain, for example, which is a model that generates a likely outcome based on a string of inputs. This is actually fairly useful in predicting weather with few variables, and that's actually how it worked.

Consider: if it's raining today, what's the likelihood of it raining *tomorrow*? If it was raining *yesterday*, does that change the likelihood of rain at all? What if it's been raining heavily for a week? Consider also the history of the region being predicted; if it rains every day in June, for example, and it's June, *and* it's been raining every day so far, can rain tomorrow be predicted? A Markov chain reduces the history to a series of tokens (which might combine the day of the year, the region, and the weather for that day) and have a set of outcomes that says "95% of the time, when the prior condition looks like *this*, the next day will look like *that*."

Markov chains are also useful for generating text; the ELIZA program[3] emulates a therapist similar to Carl Rogers, by taking significant parts of what you say to it and repeating those parts back to you, in a few different combinations.

Most Markov chains use some form of probability to calculate the transitions between states; Bayesian algorithms found a lot of use in early attempts to filter email spam, to quite a bit of success, although obviously spammers have found ways to avoid easy detection.

If probabilities don't sound like "artificial intelligence," well, that's fine, but it's generally unfair. Probabilities rule much of our lives; when we go for a drive, we look at our fuel and calculate how likely it is that we'll need to purchase more, or when, or whether we'll need to take an umbrella or a coat, after all.

---

[3] An example of ELIZA can be found at `https://web.njit.edu/~ronkowit/eliza.html`. Try it! It's fun! Beware: it might make you think of your mother.

CHAPTER 1   INTRODUCTION

AI also has a sort of "magic appeal" in how difficult it can be to understand what's going on behind an invocation. In the end, it's all math, but ... *what* math? And if it's math, well, do we *need* AI?

The answer is, as you might suspect, "it depends." "What math?" is answered by another question: "What are you trying to do?" An LLM does a lot of stemming and tokenization[4] to reduce a prompt to a series of numbers, which generates some amusing outcomes sometimes.[5] A Markov chain gauged toward weather would have *no* sensible output to an input that asked what 1+1 was—it's simply too sensitive to its problem domain.

It's also important to keep in mind that the reason we have so many models and definitions is because there are so many applications, some appropriate and some not.

It's an aphorism that "when all you have is a hammer, everything looks like a nail." As of this writing, this feels like an accusation; it's rather common to see "can we throw an AI at it?" as a response to problems that, honestly, don't need all that much computation power.

For example, in medicine, a cardiologist named Lee Goldman came up with three simple questions to try to determine if a patient was having a heart attack. His fellow doctors were sure that they, being experts, had a better set of questions and tests to evaluate a patient's status, but *actual tests* showed that Goldman's three questions were **70% better** at detecting

---

[4] Stemming and tokenization here refer to the process of reducing words to common, small forms: "machinations," for example, gets stemmed to "machin" as a reduced form, then that gets translated to a token—usually a simple number—for internal representation.

[5] A few weeks ago as of this writing, it was a meme about AI that the LLMs couldn't tell how many occurrences of the letter "R" were in the word "strawberry." To us, it's obviously three; to the LLM, however, it was counting based on the tokenized version of the word, which had two Rs, not three, and it ended up looking hopelessly confused, even when corrected.

heart attacks, *plus* they were far quicker to ask than the alternatives.[6] Using an AI to detect heart attacks might work—but as with Dr. Goldman's three questions, the simple approach might be faster, cheaper, and more effective than the shiny technology. This would be a poor application of the resources and power of AI.

That's not to say that you shouldn't use artificial intelligence, at all: it's more an observation that AI is a tool, and like most tools, it has appropriate uses and can be overused, and given the current enthusiasm around a term that few seem to understand, is **often** overused.

The Scope of This Book

This book delves into the integration of advanced AI models—including Large Language Models (LLMs), as well as audio and visual processing models—using the Spring Framework.

While LLMs transform textual prompts into meaningful textual responses through complex mathematical computations, AI's capabilities are not limited to text. In this book, you will also learn how to process and generate audio and visual data using AI models. Specifically, Chapters 4 and 5 focus on feeding audio and visual inputs into these models and retrieving corresponding outputs. By the end of this book, you'll be prepared to handle a variety of data types—textual, auditory, and visual—within your Spring Framework applications.

---

[6] Malcolm Gladwell, *Blink: The Power of Thinking without Thinking*, Back Bay Books, 2007.

CHAPTER 1   INTRODUCTION

How Can AIs Be Used?

AIs are effectively information blenders; you give them a filter (the prompt), and they generate a probabilistic outcome based on the information on which they were trained.

Therefore, selecting a model can be of critical importance. (You wouldn't want to use a model trained primarily on fantasy literature to make medical conclusions.[7])

One way to think about the output of an LLM is as if it were selected at random based on what other people *might* have said, as if the LLM were to take all of the possible answers to your prompt, stir them together and pick elements at random, and then present the result in a cohesive manner.

This is why stories written by an AI tend to be faintly familiar: they are! They're taking common elements of storytelling and replacing bits as they go, and the result can feel original at times while feeling horribly derivative at other times. That doesn't mean the story isn't worth telling—most stories in human history have a similar set of concepts at their hearts, as Joseph Campbell[8] might have told you—but it also isn't the same as coming up with "original content."

But with this observation—that AIs are stirring up knowledge we already had in possibly unexpected ways to come up with content—it's worth saying that this is *useful*.

---

[7] However, you *might* want an AI trained on a sufficient medical dataset to provide initial conclusions. AIs lack doctors' biases and can often see the problem as it is, without a doctor's presumptions or preferences factoring in. With that said, this is *not* a recommendation to avoid your doctor.

[8] Joseph Campbell wrote a book in 1949 called *The Hero with a Thousand Faces* that described a common set of concepts in human mythology, often summed up as the "Hero's Journey." See https://www.amazon.com/Thousand-Faces-Collected-Joseph-Campbell/dp/1577315936 for more.

7

CHAPTER 1   INTRODUCTION

Sometimes things we want to know are "hiding in plain sight," obscured by tradition and expectation, and an AI can abstract over arbitrarily large amounts of information; it can see common patterns that humans can overlook, and without models being specifically limited in what they can observe, an AI is able to point out the emperor's lack of clothing with ease[9] fairly easily.

For this book, ChatGPT was used as the AI of choice, and it was *also* used to evaluate content and tone. Unless specifically pointed out, the words you are reading were written by an actual human person and were evaluated by an AI to suggest revisions and additions, some of which were accepted.

How Do You Choose an AI?

That's a good question! As with others, the answer is "it depends on what you want," combined with what you want to spend and the cost of using a given AI service.

There are a lot of choices:

Name	Source	Url
ChatGPT	OpenAI	`https://chatgpt.com`
Meta	Facebook	`https://meta.ai`
Grok	X	`https://x.ai/`
Amazon Bedrock	Amazon	`https://aws.amazon.com/bedrock/`
Claude	Anthropic	`https://claude.ai/`
Ollama	Open Source	`https://ollama.com/`

---

[9] For reference, if you're unfamiliar: "The Emperor's New Clothes" is a story by Hans Christian Andersen, and a workable summary can be found online at `https://en.wikipedia.org/wiki/The_Emperor%27s_New_Clothes`.

That's just a **few** of the options.

Most of them use a similar API endpoint (after all, they do have a pretty common usage pattern), but their capabilities aren't quite the same; Ollama, for example, doesn't support audio or image generation as of this writing in and of itself, while ChatGPT certainly does.

This is actually why you'd want to use Spring AI: it abstracts much of the low-level APIs into a common framework. There are areas in which you **are** coding to a specific AI, particularly when setting the options for how it generates content, but that's **usually** it, and those features can often be set by configuration rather than being set specifically in code.

As far as choosing an AI: this book primarily focuses on using ChatGPT, because it was one of the first major vendors for AI services using a Large Language Model, and it's remarkably sufficient for a general-purpose AI without being absurdly expensive. Ollama has the benefit of running locally, if you have a sufficient GPU; it can run without a GPU, in CPU mode, but tends to result in *very* slow response times.

With that said, the main way to make a decision about which AI to use is to *try them* for your purpose.

Work out your application's purpose, write tests that submit to your AI of choice, and see how it performs against other LLMs, and balance the response time and cost against your needs.

How Much Does It Actually Cost?

The popular AIs (apart from Ollama, which runs locally, and thus is "free" outside of the cost of the hardware used to run it) have various pricing models. They're typically based on the amount of power it requires to process various prompts and types of prompts, so generating images might have a different cost based on image size and the complexity of the prompt, while text prompts only deal with the complexity of the prompt and its answer.

CHAPTER 1   INTRODUCTION

In addition to the prompts, the models used for processing have their own costs, so a high-quality, large model from a provider is likely to cost more than a simple, fast model from the same provider. There are lots of providers, each with their own pricing structures, so you should take a little time and look at the requirements you have: the pricing model for OpenAI, the host of ChatGPT and the service used most often in this book, has a pricing model that can be found at `https://openai.com/api/pricing/`.

This book uses a lot of very short AI prompts, generally, so the token counts for the entire book, added together, work out to probably under a thousand tokens.[10]

If you run the entire book's tests over and over again, that adds up, but it's still not a lot.

If you're doing a lot of detailed analysis covering a lot of data, your token counts will be higher, and you might run into costs associated with analysis; Chapter 3 covers some ways to mitigate this, but in the end, if you need a certain number of tokens to achieve a task, you… need a certain number of tokens to achieve a task, and your selection of a model and provider will be balanced against your requirements.

The short version of all of that: expect a relatively minor cost, and watch your typical usage to try to predict whether you need additional capacity or not. If you do need more capacity, consider whether you have the resources to run Ollama locally (meaning that you have a decent GPU and RAM, and a fast disk), and *try it*.

The advantage of external AI providers is that they have massive server farms to throw at tasks, meaning that you can work with larger models and expect faster response times, with more features; the disadvantages of external providers are that they can see your prompts (and how that's used is up to the provider; read the fine print!) and you have to pay for their services.

---

[10] This is a guess. We could calculate it, because interactions with an LLM include token counts in the response metadata, but for this book, it's just not worth the effort. Your mileage may vary.

What This Book Isn't

This book is going to cover a lot of code, of course, being a book about Spring AI. However, it presumes you know Java to some degree and have some familiarity with the Spring Framework (and Spring Boot) already.

It requires you to have Java and Maven installed, although handy links will be provided just in case you don't.[11]

This book does **not** require an IDE. You'll want one, we think, but ... which one? We don't know, and don't care. You can use a simple text editor, if that's what you desire, or IDEA, or Eclipse (or the Spring Tool Suite, which is based on Eclipse), or NetBeans, or Visual Studio Code; we offer these names as they occurred to us to write, not as an indication of preference in any way.

The book also generally focuses on tests as a way to demonstrate technique. There are a few places where there's an application to execute (particularly in Chapter 4, which provides a web-based application to convert text to speech), but the *primary* demonstration is in setting expectations of output given a specific set of inputs and validation of that output.

When the code compiles and the tests pass, the code works. Otherwise, there's not a lot to demonstrate, so there aren't a lot of screenshots to look for. (Given the nature of probabilistic outputs from LLMs, though, there are places where you might be expected to look at a generated string to make sure it fits your expectations, although we're generally trying to avoid this.)

---

[11] Your authors have no idea why books on programming have to walk through basic things like "installing your language of choice," but if you don't have some of that, the technical reviewers whine about it.

CHAPTER 1 INTRODUCTION

It's also not a book that's exhaustively going to cover every AI technique—or even every possibility of how to work with a given AI model. It's focused on the most common applications of AI, and other applications and models are more advanced topics that are better covered by other materials.[12]

LLMs have different capabilities and settings; part of why we chose ChatGPT was because ChatGPT covers the features that most people want, and other AIs may or may not provide the same set of features, but few other AIs provide features ChatGPT does *not*. Readers who wish to use alternatives should be able to fine-tune the example code for their specific AI implementation without too much effort. (And if it takes a lot of effort, feel free to reach out to your authors; we're very interested in helping the industry move forward!)

We're also not covering exhaustive techniques in terms of how the AIs are being interacted with. Most of the uses of AI are through simple back-and-forth conversations, and while we *will* be covering "conversations," we're not going into streaming techniques that have things like LLMs feed back information *as it's being generated*—this is useful for emulating human behavior ("See, it's typing right now!") but complicates the interactions drastically, and complicated code tends to hide the intent behind what the code is doing.

Next Steps

In our next chapter, we're going to walk through setting up a project that includes calling ChatGPT through Spring AI.[13]

---

[12] Honest truth: Your author considered having an AI rewrite that sentence.

[13] It would not be difficult to use any other AI provider, but again, this book uses ChatGPT, because it's very common, well known, and very predictable—and it definitely provides all of the services the book covers.

CHAPTER 2

Getting Started

The Project Structure

This book is organized as a single Maven[1] project, using Java 21.[2] Installing these tools is beyond the scope of this book; consider asking tools like ChatGPT for advice for your operating system!

Maven uses a fairly verbose object model, written with XML, to describe projects. This was chosen here because it involves *fewer* files (a pom.xml can describe a project completely) and Maven has demonstrated excellent compatibility across versions, whereas Gradle—the other popular build tool for the JVM—has much shorter build scripts but uses *multiple* build scripts for each project, and it's focused more on feature sets than compatibility.

We don't have a preference between Maven or Gradle in reality, but in a book, tool stability is *critical*.

---

[1] Maven can be found at https://maven.apache.org/. It's one of the two most popular build tools for the JVM ecosystem.

[2] As this book is being written, Java 21 is the current release of Java with long-term support. There are lots of ways to download Java, but which one is best depends on your skill level and operating system. In a pinch, you can find it at https://jdk.java.net/21, but readers of this book are likely to already have a JVM installed. We only included this footnote because *every other book* has stuff on installing tools and we didn't want to feel left out.

CHAPTER 2 GETTING STARTED

This book's project is called bsai-code. It contains *modules*, named after each chapter, so the top-level project contains modules named chapter02, chapter03, and so forth. The top-level project serves to centralize the dependencies that **every** module needs, which means that in our case it makes sure the Spring dependencies are consistent.

Each chapter has a directory structure, an effective standard across Java projects, that looks like this.

Listing 2-1. The standard Maven directory structure

```
.
./src
./src/main/java
./src/main/resources
./src/test/java
./src/test/resources
```

This can be created in the "project directory" with the following command, if you're running a POSIX shell like bash or zsh.

Listing 2-2. Creating the project directory structure in POSIX

```
mkdir -p src/{main,test}/{java,resources}
```

This is all fairly standard for Java programmers; it's being included here for completeness more than anything else. Project listings are offsets from the "book's project directory," so the following listing is in the "top level" directory.

Listing 2-3. pom.xml

```xml
<?xml version="1.0" encoding="UTF-8"?>
<project xmlns="http://maven.apache.org/POM/4.0.0"
         xmlns:xsi="http://www.w3.org/2001/XMLSchema-instance"
         xsi:schemaLocation="http://maven.apache.org/POM/4.0.0
```

```xml
            http://maven.apache.org/xsd/maven-4.0.0.xsd">
<modelVersion>4.0.0</modelVersion>
<parent>
    <groupId>org.springframework.boot</groupId>
    <artifactId>spring-boot-starter-parent</artifactId>
    <version>3.3.0</version>
    <relativePath/> <!-- lookup parent from repository -->
</parent>

<groupId>com.apress</groupId>
<artifactId>bsai-code</artifactId>
<version>1.0</version>
<packaging>pom</packaging>

<modules>
    <module>chapter02</module>
    <module>chapter03</module>
    <module>chapter04</module>
    <module>chapter05</module>
</modules>

<properties>
    <project.build.sourceEncoding>UTF-8</project.build.sourceEncoding>
    <java.version>21</java.version>
    <spring-ai.version>1.0.0.M2</spring-ai.version>
    <kotlin.version>2.0.20</kotlin.version>
</properties>

<dependencyManagement>
    <dependencies>
        <dependency>
            <groupId>org.springframework.ai</groupId>
            <artifactId>spring-ai-bom</artifactId>
```

```xml
            <version>${spring-ai.version}</version>
            <type>pom</type>
            <scope>import</scope>
        </dependency>
    </dependencies>
</dependencyManagement>

<dependencies>
    <dependency>
        <groupId>org.jetbrains.kotlin</groupId>
        <artifactId>kotlin-stdlib-jdk8</artifactId>
        <version>${kotlin.version}</version>
    </dependency>
    <dependency>
        <groupId>org.jetbrains.kotlin</groupId>
        <artifactId>kotlin-test</artifactId>
        <version>${kotlin.version}</version>
        <scope>test</scope>
    </dependency>
</dependencies>

<build>
    <plugins>
        <plugin>
            <groupId>org.springframework.boot</groupId>
            <artifactId>spring-boot-maven-plugin
            </artifactId>
            <configuration>
                <skip>true</skip>
            </configuration>
        </plugin>
```

```xml
<plugin>
    <groupId>org.apache.maven.plugins</groupId>
    <artifactId>maven-surefire-plugin</artifactId>
    <version>3.3.0</version>
</plugin>
<plugin>
    <groupId>org.jetbrains.kotlin</groupId>
    <artifactId>kotlin-maven-plugin</artifactId>
    <version>${kotlin.version}</version>
    <executions>
        <execution>
            <id>compile</id>
            <phase>compile</phase>
            <goals>
                <goal>compile</goal>
            </goals>
        </execution>
        <execution>
            <id>test-compile</id>
            <phase>test-compile</phase>
            <goals>
                <goal>test-compile</goal>
            </goals>
        </execution>
    </executions>
    <configuration>
        <jvmTarget>1.8</jvmTarget>
    </configuration>
</plugin>
    </plugins>
</build>
```

```xml
    <repositories>
        <repository>
            <id>spring-milestones</id>
            <name>Spring Milestones</name>
            <url>https://repo.spring.io/milestone</url>
            <snapshots>
                <enabled>false</enabled>
            </snapshots>
        </repository>
        <repository>
            <id>spring-snapshots</id>
            <name>Spring Snapshots</name>
            <url>https://repo.spring.io/snapshot</url>
            <releases>
                <enabled>false</enabled>
            </releases>
        </repository>
    </repositories>
</project>
```

This is *this chapter's* project file, and thus it's in a directory *under* the top-level directory, called chapter02, and the file is named pom.xml. It's fairly straightforward in and of itself, including the dependencies we need to access Spring AI: the OpenAI starter (spring-ai-openai-spring-boot-starter), spring-boot-starter-web because we need some classes from it to provide services for OpenAI, a test starter (spring-boot-starter-test, excluding an android JSON library because we don't need it and Spring will warn us about duplication otherwise), and commons-math3, because we'll want to use some simple mathematics operations later in this chapter and we don't want to have to write the code ourselves.

Listing 2-4. chapter02/pom.xml

```xml
<?xml version="1.0" encoding="UTF-8"?>

<project xmlns="http://maven.apache.org/POM/4.0.0"
        xmlns:xsi="http://www.w3.org/2001/XMLSchema-instance"
        xsi:schemaLocation="http://maven.apache.org/POM/4.0.0
        http://maven.apache.org/xsd/maven-4.0.0.xsd">
    <modelVersion>4.0.0</modelVersion>
    <parent>
        <groupId>com.apress</groupId>
        <artifactId>bsai-code</artifactId>
        <version>1.0</version>
    </parent>

    <artifactId>chapter02</artifactId>
    <version>1.0</version>

    <properties>
    </properties>

    <dependencies>
        <dependency>
            <groupId>org.springframework.ai</groupId>
            <artifactId>spring-ai-openai-spring-boot-starter
            </artifactId>
        </dependency>
        <dependency>
            <groupId>org.springframework.boot</groupId>
            <artifactId>spring-boot-starter-web</artifactId>
        </dependency>
        <dependency>
            <groupId>org.springframework.boot</groupId>
            <artifactId>spring-boot-starter-test</artifactId>
```

```xml
            <scope>test</scope>
            <exclusions>
                <exclusion>
                    <groupId>com.vaadin.external.google
                    </groupId>
                    <artifactId>android-json</artifactId>
                </exclusion>
            </exclusions>
        </dependency>
        <dependency>
            <groupId>org.apache.commons</groupId>
            <artifactId>commons-math3</artifactId>
            <version>3.6.1</version>
        </dependency>
        <dependency>
            <groupId>org.apache.commons</groupId>
            <artifactId>commons-text</artifactId>
            <version>1.12.0</version>
        </dependency>
        <dependency>
            <groupId>com.google.guava</groupId>
            <artifactId>guava</artifactId>
            <version>33.2.1-jre</version>
        </dependency>
    </dependencies>
</project>
```

Note The dependency on `spring-boot-starter-web` is due to the way the Spring AI modules are being developed. As this book was being written, there was an implicit requirement for classes in the

CHAPTER 2   GETTING STARTED

web module, as opposed to an *explicit* transient requirement, so we have to include this on our own. By the time *you* use Spring AI, this requirement may have changed.

We'll want one more file to save ourselves a lot of unnecessary duplication: an .env file. This file is going to hold our OpenAI access key. This is a token provided by OpenAI to keep track of usage and capabilities, and we'll detail how to get it in the next section of this chapter; most of the providers have a similar value, and getting their access keys may differ slightly. In each case, however, this is a simple name/value pair, and this file goes into the root of our project structure.

Listing 2-5. .env

```
OPENAI_API_KEY=[your-api-key-value-here]
```

Thus, we should have a project structure that looks like this, so far.

Listing 2-6. The project structure early in Chapter 2

```
> tree
.
├── .env
├── chapter02
│   ├── pom.xml
│   └── src
│       ├── main
│       │   ├── java
│       │   └── resources
│       └── test
│           ├── java
│           └── resources
└── pom.xml
```

CHAPTER 2   GETTING STARTED

All that's very exciting and good, but it's time to actually write some code and show some basic functionality.

Spring AI

Spring AI builds around the idea of a *Model*. A model accepts a request and feeds back a response in some format; chat models use text, and there are also image models and audio models. There's even a model *abstraction* to provide for mechanisms that haven't necessarily been anticipated yet.[3]

There are variants for even the coarse abstractions: a chat model, for example, has a blocking version and a streaming version, where the blocking version returns a "complete answer" and the streaming version returns the answer in intermediate steps, much as a human would as they type out a response.

In simplest form, to use Spring AI, you acquire a model, with appropriate configuration to inform the model of what sources to use, and issue a call to get the response. That sounds so simple that we should build something and test it out.

Note   We've chosen to use OpenAI for the base service for this book. As Chapter 1 mentioned, this is a commercial service; you'll need to set up an API key for use, and in the process of running the examples in this book, you *will* consume resources on OpenAI that may incur a cost. This was done because OpenAI is commercial and *predictable*. We know the resources it has available. Ollama is free

---

[3] Imagine an AI that responds with peanut butter and jelly sandwiches! … or don't, we don't mind.

CHAPTER 2   GETTING STARTED

but has very high demands in terms of hardware; it is **certainly** possible to use Ollama instead of OpenAI, but we chose to focus on reproducible results for the reader; OpenAI tends to be faster and doesn't rely on the reader having a relatively high-end CPU/GPU combination with plenty of disk space.

We need to build a configuration first. This is done in two places: the .env file mentioned in the prior section (see Listing 2-5) and in a Spring configuration class.

Getting the OpenAI Key

To get your OpenAI key, you'll need to go to https://platform.openai.com/ and create an account. From there, you'll go to "Settings"—the gear on the page—and see this screen:

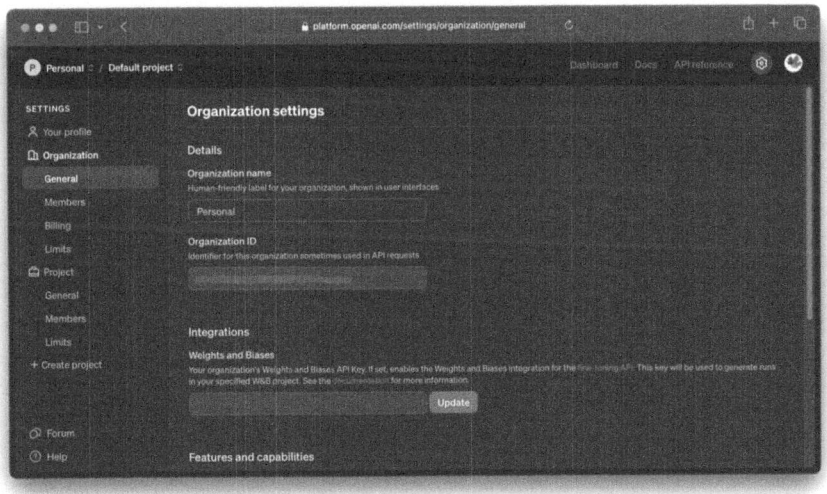

The OpenAI settings screen

23

CHAPTER 2   GETTING STARTED

We need to use a *project key*, so select "Create project" in the menu on the left hand side of the page.

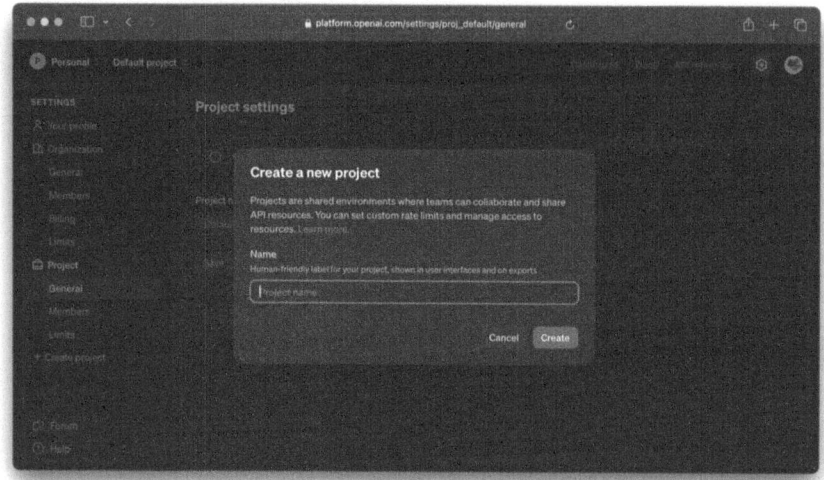

Creating a project on OpenAI.com

Enter a project name that makes sense for you (we chose "Beginning Spring AI"), and you'll see a page with a *project key* on it, like this:

CHAPTER 2   GETTING STARTED

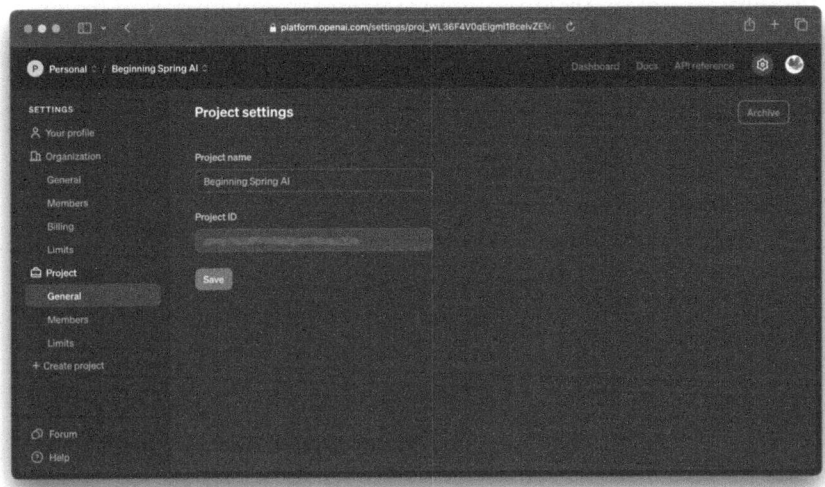

The Project settings on OpenAI.com

The next thing we need to do is create an API key. In the profile, it gives you a chance to manage the permissions for various keys; as this is being written, this defaults to managing the API keys *per user*, but this is being deprecated for the use of *project keys*.

Warning   This is all under active development, so the user interface may have changed since this was written.

Select the project in the top of the window (where we have "Beginning Spring AI"), and you'll see an option for "API keys" on the right side. Selecting this link gives you a chance to create new secrets—the API keys you need. When you generate these, save them somewhere safe—and use set the value in the .env file for use by Spring AI. The value you'll want should look like sk-proj- followed by a number of other letters.

If you lose this key, all you need to do is create a new one—but OpenAI doesn't show you the keys again, so keep track of it.

CHAPTER 2   GETTING STARTED

The value in the "Project ID" field is what we'll put in the .env file.

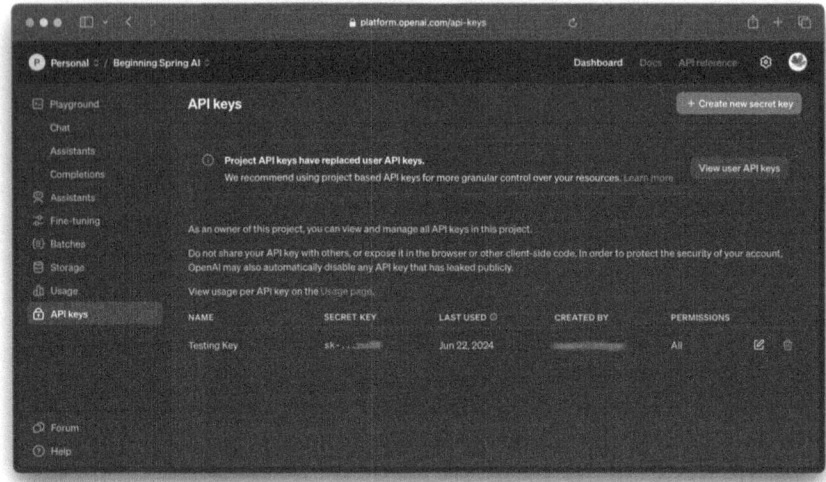

The API settings page

That's a lot of setup! Thankfully, we won't need to do it more than once for this book, unless the original secret key is lost. It's time to code.

Our First OpenAI Query

The first thing we need to handle in any Spring application is the application configuration itself. Spring has a lot of very flexible approaches to configuration, and those approaches deserve their own book.[4] We're going to use a simple approach to Spring configuration, so our application will look as simple as possible.

---

[4] In fact, Spring configuration not only deserves its own book, but there are multiple books that cover Spring configuration very well.

Listing 2-7. chapter02/src/main/java/ch02/Ch02Configuration.java

```java
package ch02;

import org.springframework.boot.autoconfigure.SpringBootApplication;

@SpringBootApplication
public class Ch02Configuration {
}
```

That's it. We're going to use `@Service` to mark resources that Spring will scan and configure for us. With that said, it's time to look at how Spring AI's `ChatClient` actually works.

A `ChatClient` uses a `Prompt` to interact with the language model. A `Prompt` might be as simple as a block of text but can configure what model is being used, the accepted variability of the response, and a host of other options. These can be controlled at the point of the request, in code, but we can also control them in our application properties. We'll need to set the API key, in any event, so let's take a look at some of the more useful properties we can set for Spring AI. (Spring has many, *many* settings available, depending on what modules you choose to use; we're *only* looking at Spring AI here.)

Property name	Description
`spring.ai.openai.api-key`	The API key to be used by the application
`spring.ai.openai.chat.options.temperature`	This determines the variability of the responses. A high temperature means the model generates more diverse answers, and a low temperature means the answers are more deterministic.
`spring.ai.openai.chat.options.model`	This is the name of the model to use. This addresses the *type* of trainings used as well as the *cost* of the trainings used. The model names, and their prices, can be found at `https://openai.com/api/pricing/`; see Chapter 1 for more discussion of how this is relevant and how it's calculated.

Note Astute readers will see the use of `openai` in those properties. Each specific Spring AI implementation has its own variation of these values; if you're using Ollama, for example, you'd set the default model with `spring.ai.ollama.chat.options.model` instead.

There are certainly more options that can be played with, of course, and we'll cover them as needed.

Typically, we're going to center on an inexpensive and relatively low-powered model (`gpt-3.5-turbo`) for this book, because we're more concerned with how the Spring AI API works *with* the models, rather than being concerned with the output of the models themselves.

We need to at least provide the API key to our chapter's code, and we want the model to be as deterministic as possible for now, so here's our `application.properties`. This is all very test-centric, so we're

CHAPTER 2   GETTING STARTED

going to place it in chapter02/src/test/resources. Note the use of spring.config.import, which allows us to load our .env file's values for internal use.

Listing 2-8. chapter02/src/test/resources/application.properties

```
spring.config.import=file:../.env[.properties]
```

```
spring.ai.openai.api-key=${OPENAI_API_KEY}
spring.ai.openai.chat.options.temperature=0.0
spring.ai.openai.chat.options.model=gpt-3.5-turbo
spring.ai.retry.max-attempts=4
```

Let's take a look at a simple chat "client"—a test that demonstrates how we might wish to interact with class that uses Spring AI. (We're going to look at the client next, we promise.)

This test is fundamentally simple: it loads the Spring configuration for testing and issues a simple request to OpenAI. We're going to ask a question about the speed of a particular kind of boat carrying tea in a specific body of water; we don't care about the **actual response**, but given that we're setting spring.ai.openai.chat.options.temperature to 0.0, we expect the answers to be pretty consistent across requests, and we can example the output for expected values to determine if the query response is "right."

Listing 2-9. chapter02/src/test/java/ch02/Ch02FirstTests.java

```
package ch02;

import ch02.service.FirstChatService;
import org.junit.jupiter.api.Test;
import org.slf4j.Logger;
import org.slf4j.LoggerFactory;
import org.springframework.beans.factory.annotation.Autowired;
import org.springframework.boot.test.context.SpringBootTest;

import static org.junit.jupiter.api.Assertions.assertTrue;
```

CHAPTER 2   GETTING STARTED

```java
@SpringBootTest(webEnvironment = SpringBootTest.WebEnvironment.MOCK)
public class FirstTests {
    private final Logger log = LoggerFactory.getLogger(this.getClass());
    @Autowired
    FirstChatService firstChatService;

    @Test
    void runSimpleQuery() {
        var response = firstChatService.query(
                "what is the speed of a typical junk carrying tea in November?\n" +
                "Assume clear weather and standard currents in the south China sea."
        );
        log.info(response);
        assertTrue(response.toLowerCase().contains("south china sea"));
    }
}
```

For the record, the response OpenAI gave for this prompt as this chapter was being written was: "The speed of a typical junk carrying tea in November in the South China Sea can vary depending on various factors such as the size of the junk, the wind conditions, and the currents. However, on average, junks can travel at speeds ranging from 5 to 10 knots (5.75 to 11.5 mph) in calm weather conditions."

This is mildly fascinating in and of itself, but note how we're having to phrase the query. This book isn't about writing efficient or effective queries, but we're going to modify how this prompt is constructed to make it a little more targeted for our purposes over time.

Of course, we can't *run* this yet, because we don't have `FirstChatService` implemented.

Our `FirstChatService` has one public method in it, `query(String)`, which returns a `String`. This method represents the *essential* mechanism that *every call in Spring AI will follow*, although there are a lot of variations we can apply.

First we have to have a `Client` available (in this case, a `ChatClient`). We'll use Spring's dependency injection to get a `ChatClient.Builder` provided, as one is automatically provided by Spring AI.

Next, to issue a call, we build a `Prompt`; there are a number of variations here, but we're going to use the simplest first, and rely on the default options from `application.properties` to determine temperature and model.

Once we have a prompt, we issue a call to the API, whether blocking or streaming; in this case, we don't care about streaming, so we use `call()` to get the response specification.

Once we have the response specification, we can get the simple content by using the `content()` method; this is a short form of `getResult().getOutput().getContent()`. If we wanted to, we could get metadata about the call like the number of tokens consumed on our API key and a few other interesting elements.

This sounds pretty straightforward, so let's see what the actual Java class looks like.

Listing 2-10. chapter02/src/main/java/ch02/service/FirstChatService.java

```java
package ch02.service;

import org.springframework.ai.chat.client.ChatClient;
import org.springframework.ai.chat.prompt.Prompt;
import org.springframework.stereotype.Service;
```

CHAPTER 2 GETTING STARTED

```java
import java.util.Objects;

@Service
public class FirstChatService {
    protected final ChatClient client;

    FirstChatService(ChatClient.Builder builder) {
        this.client = builder.build();
    }

    public final String query(String query) {
        Objects.requireNonNull(query);

        var prompt = new Prompt(query);

        var request = client
                .prompt(prompt);

        var responseSpecification = request.call();

        return responseSpecification.content();
    }
}
```

Now we actually have something we can test. We can run this chapter's test suite by using Maven:

```
mvn -am -pl chapter02 clean test
```

If everything works properly, we should see output that looks something like this screenshot, in part:

The output from Ch02FirstTests

Choosing a Different Model

The model being specified here is, as mentioned, gpt-3.5-turbo, which is an inexpensive, somewhat dated model. There are *many* different models to choose from, with the "most current" on OpenAI being the gpt-4o model. We could set it as the default in application.properties, but we can also provide options to the Prompt and set it there. Let's see that in action, with a OptionChatService that allows us to provide ChatOptions, and then we'll show a test that uses it.

Listing 2-11. chapter02/src/main/java/ch02/service/OptionChatService.java

```java
package ch02.service;

import org.springframework.ai.chat.client.ChatClient;
import org.springframework.ai.chat.prompt.Prompt;
import org.springframework.ai.openai.OpenAiChatOptions;
import org.springframework.stereotype.Service;

import java.util.Objects;

@Service
public class OptionChatService extends FirstChatService {
    OptionChatService(ChatClient.Builder builder) {
        super(builder);
    }

    public final String query(String query, OpenAiChatOptions options) {
        Objects.requireNonNull(options);
        Objects.requireNonNull(query);

        var prompt = new Prompt(query, options);
```

```
        var request = client
                .prompt(prompt);

        var responseSpecification = request.call();

        return responseSpecification.content();
    }
}
```

This overloads the query method from FirstChatService to also accept an OpenAiChatOptions instance. To use it, all we have to do is pass it to the creation of the Prompt. After that, the call follows the same pattern as we saw in FirstChatService to the letter.

As with the openai properties in our configuration file, different Spring AI libraries have different capabilities. We're targeting OpenAI here, but there are variants for the other LLM implementations that reflect the options those services provide. There is a ChatOptions object that exposes generalized parameters—like temperature—but not every LLM allows us to select a model on the fly like OpenAI does, so we're going to limit ourselves to the OpenAiChatOptions type here.

Astute readers might wish to invert the service' calls, such that query(String) constructs a default ChatOptions and passes it to the more flexible query(String, OpenAiChatOptions) method. This makes a lot of sense, and in a "real project" that would certainly be advisable—but in a "real project" you wouldn't have multiple instances like this. This code is being constructed for the purpose of education, not an example to follow.[5]

Let's show this in action, and let's set the model to gpt-4o. There are other options we can set—temperature, for example—and we'll see that next. Let's keep ourselves looking at the model for now.

---

[5] It's not an example to follow *unless you're writing your own book*, we suppose, and if you follow our example *there*, consider us flattered.

Listing 2-12. chapter02/src/test/java/ch02/Ch02OptionTests.java

```java
package ch02;

import ch02.service.OptionChatService;
import org.junit.jupiter.api.Test;
import org.slf4j.Logger;
import org.slf4j.LoggerFactory;
import org.springframework.ai.openai.OpenAiChatOptions;
import org.springframework.beans.factory.annotation.Autowired;
import org.springframework.boot.test.context.SpringBootTest;

import static org.junit.jupiter.api.Assertions.assertTrue;

@SpringBootTest(webEnvironment = SpringBootTest.WebEnvironment.MOCK)
public class OptionTests {
    private final Logger log = LoggerFactory.getLogger(this.getClass());
    @Autowired
    OptionChatService optionChatService;

    @Test
    void runSimpleQuery() {
        var response = optionChatService.query(
                "what is the speed of a typical junk carrying tea in November?\n" +
                "Assume clear weather and standard currents in the south China sea.",
                OpenAiChatOptions.builder()
                        .withModel("gpt-4o")
                        .build()
        );
```

CHAPTER 2 GETTING STARTED

```
        log.info(response);
        assertTrue(response.toLowerCase().contains("south
        china sea"));
    }
}
```

If you're writing the code yourself as we go through the book, the command to execute all of the tests in this chapter is:

```
mvn -am -pl chapter02 clean test
```

The output for this execution is relatively variable (thanks to the default temperature of queries), but one run locally generated this output[6]:

The speed of a typical junk (a traditional Chinese sailing ship) carrying tea in the South China Sea can vary based on several factors, including the design of the junk, the skill of the crew, and the specific weather and sea conditions. However, under clear weather and standard currents, a traditional junk might typically travel at speeds ranging from 4 to 8 knots (approximately 4.6 to 9.2 miles per hour or 7.4 to 14.8 kilometers per hour).

It's important to note that these speeds are general estimates and can vary. Modern adaptations or motorized junks could achieve different speeds.

---

[6] We're going to stick on the subject of junks, which are, according to Wikipedia, "a type of Chinese sailing ship characterized by a central rudder, an overhanging flat transom, watertight bulkheads, and a flat-bottomed design." The subject was chosen mostly to avoid referring to African laden swallows, which—let's be real—nobody cares about.

Temperature

We've described temperature as "determining the variability of the responses" from a language model. It turns out that there are two parameters that have similar effects on how an LLM generates content: one is `temperature`, and the other is `top_p`, which refers to "probability mass." Both refer to how content is selected by the LLM.

Lower `top_p` and `temperature` values indicate less variability in the responses. The ranges for the values are slightly different: `top_p` refers to a percentage of things to consider (so `0.10` means "consider the most relevant tokens" and `1.0` would mean "don't filter tokens at all"), and `temperature` refers to how tokens are selected, with a range from `0.0` to `2.0`, where `2.0` indicates very high variability.

One would use *either* `top_p` or `temperature`—you don't normally use them both. (However, it's not going to be a programmatic error to *set* them both—the documentation isn't clear on what happens in the service itself when both are used.)

Specifying either one is trivial: in the code where we build the `OpenAiChatOptions`, simply include a `temperature` value, for example:

```
var options=OpenAiChatOptions.builder()
    .withModel("gpt-4o")
    .withTemperature(1.0f)
    .build();
```

We use the archaic `1.0f` form for the float because Java is strongly typed, and the actual parameter is a `Float`—which the compiler won't normally translate `1.0`, a `double`, to a `Float` for us. Normally, Java's strong typing works in our favor, but the use of `Float` in the API makes this slightly problematic, if by "problematic" we mean that we have to use the narrower type.

There are two questions to ask here: one is "What does this mean for our code?" and the other is "What actual impact does it have?"—with the latter question being more important.

It's not easy to answer, in a concrete sense. Both `temperature` and `top_p` serve as inputs for the language model, basically "churning the water" for output. The `top_p` parameter, for example, controls what elements are selected for generating output: if you imagined a list of colors ordered by popularity, `top_p` might provide a way to suggest selecting the *more popular* colors rather than the colors at random (by limiting the selection to the "top colors," so to speak.) Temperature also refers to how things are selected in the model.

As a result, a higher `temperature` or `top_p` value provides a wider range of inputs for the generation of a response, which makes it "more variable."

So how do we **measure** this, such that we can demonstrate it?

What we need to do is have a way to describe similarity between blocks of text. This is, luckily for us, a known thing. There are *lots* of ways to measure similarity, but we're going to use a simple one, called a Jaccard similarity, which is basically a measure of the number of common elements between two sets against the measure of elements that they *don't* have in common.[7]

To build the corpus, the body text, for similarity, we're going to extract n-grams from text; n-grams are sequences of tokens in a specific order. An example of a set of n-grams of length two from the, well, definition of n-grams might look like this:

```
n-grams are
```

---

[7] To learn more about Jaccard similarity, see https://www.learndatasci.com/glossary/jaccard-similarity/—and there are **definitely** other ways to measure similarities between texts, but a Jaccard similarity is effective enough for our purposes **and** it's relatively little code, so you're not having to pore through seven pages of Lucene example code.

```
are sequences
sequences of
of tokens
tokens in
in a
a specific
specific order
```

If you built n-grams of length three, you'd get this set:

```
n-grams are sequences
are sequences of
sequences of tokens
of tokens in
tokens in a
in a specific
a specific order
```

We can compare the set of n-grams generated from "constant" queries—queries with very low `temperature` or `top_p` values—and compare them to queries with higher variability. If our supposition is correct—that the higher values have higher variability—we should see **increasing** variations in those sets of n-grams over time.

Let's create a Spring bean to give us a Jaccard similarity score.

Listing 2-13. chapter02/src/main/java/ch02/service/JaccardSimilarityCalculator.java

```
package ch02.service;
```

```
import org.springframework.stereotype.Service;
```

```
import java.util.*;
```

```
@Service
```

```java
public class JaccardSimilarityCalculator {
    public double calculateJaccardSimilarity(String text1,
    String text2, int ngramSize) {
        // Preprocess texts
        Set<String> set1 = new HashSet<>(preprocessText(text1,
        ngramSize));
        Set<String> set2 = new HashSet<>(preprocessText(text2,
        ngramSize));

        // Calculate intersection
        Set<String> intersection = new HashSet<>(set1);
        intersection.retainAll(set2);

        // Calculate union
        Set<String> union = new HashSet<>(set1);
        union.addAll(set2);

        // Calculate Jaccard similarity
        return (double) intersection.size() / union.size();
    }

    private Set<String> preprocessText(String text, int
    ngramSize) {
        String[] tokens=text.toLowerCase().split("\\W+");
        Set<String> ngrams = new HashSet<>();
        for (int i = 0; i <= tokens.length - ngramSize; i++) {
            StringBuilder ngram = new StringBuilder();
            for (int j = 0; j < ngramSize; j++) {
                ngram.append(tokens[i + j]).append(" ");
            }
            ngrams.add(ngram.toString().trim());
        }
        return ngrams;
    }
}
```

This is fairly easy to demonstrate, and we don't trust code without tests—or we shouldn't—so let's see it in action, before we apply it to our conversations with an LLM.

Listing 2-14. chapter02/src/test/java/ch02/JaccardTests.java

```java
package ch02;

import ch02.service.JaccardSimilarityCalculator;
import org.junit.jupiter.params.ParameterizedTest;
import org.junit.jupiter.params.provider.Arguments;
import org.junit.jupiter.params.provider.MethodSource;
import org.springframework.beans.factory.annotation.Autowired;
import org.springframework.boot.test.context.SpringBootTest;

import java.util.stream.Stream;

import static org.junit.jupiter.api.Assertions.assertEquals;

@SpringBootTest
public class JaccardTests {
    @Autowired
    JaccardSimilarityCalculator calculator;

    public static Stream<Arguments> texts() {
        return Stream.of(
                Arguments.of(
                        "This is some cool text. More is better
                        but this will do.",
                        "This is some cool text. More is better
                        but this will do.",
                        1.0),
                Arguments.of(
                        "Now is the time for all good men to
                        come to the aid of their country.",
```

```
                        "The quick brown fox jumped over the
                        lazy dog's tail.",
                        0.0),
                Arguments.of(
                        "This is some cool text. More is better
                        but this will do.",
                        "This is some cool text. More is better
                        but this might do.",
                        0.7)
                );
    }

    @ParameterizedTest
    @MethodSource("texts")
    public void testTexts(String text1, String text2, double
    expected) {
        var similarity = calculator.calculateJaccardSimilarity(
        text1, text2,2);
        assertEquals(expected, similarity, 0.1);
    }
}
```

Here, we have a *parameterized test*, a JUnit feature that allows us to specify a list of arguments that we can throw at a single method. We have three sets of data: one set is a comparison of identical texts, that should have a *very high similarity*, and another set of texts (that we typed very quickly, thank you very much) that have relatively little similarity. Their n-grams are just too different, which is what we expect.

The similarity of 1.0 for the first input means those texts are likely to be identical (as, in fact, they are, but similarity scores *usually* trim out things like incidental words and punctuation, which we're not quite doing here).

The similarity score of `0.00` means that the second set of inputs are very different, as we expect, since the number of common n-grams is very low.

Our last test has **one word** of difference—`this will do` and `this might do`—which means we have two n-grams that differ. Here are the n-grams (with a size of 3) for those last two inputs:

First input	Second input	Same?
this is some	this is some	yes
is some cool	is some cool	yes
some cool text	some cool text	yes
cool text more	cool text more	yes
text more is	text more is	yes
more is better	more is better	yes
is better but	is better but	yes
better but this	better but this	yes
but this will	but this might	no
this will do	this might do	no

Anyway, *now* we have a pattern that we can use to throw at an LLM, with different `temperature` and `top_p` values, and we can measure those parameters' effect on the results.[8]

Our methodology here is relatively simple. We're going to test both `top_p` and `temperature`, increasing the value for multiple queries, and measure the similarity to our initial response.

---

[8] And you readers probably thought we just wanted to type "Jaccard" out a lot, to show off, didn't you?

What we *expect* is that the first test (the initial response, compared to the initial response) is *very similar* (as it should be, being the same content), and as we increase the `temperature`, our similarity score should decrease. We don't *know* that it will decrease, because that's how sampling mechanisms work—we might just *happen* to get an identical response by random chance—but we expect that overall the similarity should decrease.

With `top_p` it's a lot harder to measure, because of the nature of our query, but we're going to try anyway—we expect the slope to be *close to 0 or negative* but not necessarily negative, because `top_p` really changes the selection set for the data and not the *variability* of the data the way `temperature` does—but we're going to take a look at it anyway.

We use a `SimpleRegression` to calculate the slope of the similarity to measure this. The way this works is that we basically plot the similarity score along an X/Y axis; the "sample number" is the X axis and the "similarity" is the Y axis. We expect the numbers to go down along the X axis; thus, we expect a negative slope, **even if** a given point along the X axis is higher than its precedent.

Let's take a look at our actual test.

Listing 2-15. chapter02/src/test/java/ch02/VariabilityTests.java

```java
package ch02;

import ch02.service.JaccardSimilarityCalculator;
import ch02.service.OptionChatService;
import org.apache.commons.math3.stat.regression.SimpleRegression;
import org.junit.jupiter.params.ParameterizedTest;
import org.junit.jupiter.params.provider.Arguments;
import org.junit.jupiter.params.provider.MethodSource;
import org.slf4j.Logger;
import org.slf4j.LoggerFactory;
import org.springframework.ai.openai.OpenAiChatOptions;
```

```java
import org.springframework.beans.factory.annotation.Autowired;
import org.springframework.boot.test.context.SpringBootTest;

import java.util.ArrayList;
import java.util.stream.Stream;

import static org.apache.commons.lang3.StringUtils.*;
import static org.junit.jupiter.api.Assertions.assertTrue;

@SpringBootTest(webEnvironment = SpringBootTest.WebEnvironment.MOCK)
public class VariabilityTests {
    private final Logger log = LoggerFactory.getLogger(this.getClass());
    @Autowired
    JaccardSimilarityCalculator calculator;
    @Autowired
    OptionChatService optionChatService;

    String query = "Write a story about a salamander learning to fly.";

    public static Stream<Arguments> controlParameters() {
        return Stream.of(
                Arguments.of(true, 0.0f, 2.0f),
                Arguments.of(false, 0.01f, 0.3f)
        );
    }

    @ParameterizedTest
    @MethodSource("controlParameters")
    void testTemperatures(boolean temp, float lower, float upper) {
        var results = new ArrayList<String>();
```

```
var regression = new SimpleRegression();
// we're going to reuse the same options instance, but
change its parameters.
var options = OpenAiChatOptions.builder().build();
for (float value = lower; value < upper; value +=
(upper - lower) / 7) {
    if (temp) {
        options.setTemperature(value);
    } else {
        options.setTopP(value);
    }
    var result=optionChatService.query(query, options);
    /*
    If you'd like to see what's generated by the AI,
    uncomment the following line. Be prepared for
    a lot of content, though.
     */
    // System.out.println(result);
    results.add(result);
}
for (int i = 1; i < results.size(); i++) {
    var c = calculator.calculateJaccardSimilarity(
            results.getFirst(),
            results.get(i),
            2);
    log.info("{}: {}", graph(c), c);
    regression.addData(i, c);
}
```

CHAPTER 2 GETTING STARTED

```
        var slope = regression.getSlope();
        // slope should be negative to indicate less
        similarity...
        // although top_p is less predictable here
        log.info("Slope: {}", slope);
        assertTrue(slope < (temp ? 0.0 : 0.05));
    }

    private String graph(double c) {
        return rightPad(repeat("*", (int) (c * 20)), 22, " ");
    }
}
```

When we run this, we get a happy little graph of stars that demonstrate the similarity. The numbers will vary quite a bit based on each individual run; it's *quite possible* that you might get a test failure because the LLM just happens to generate some outputs with higher similarities. With that said, though, we haven't gotten many actual test failures based on the similarities going up.

Note With that said, we *have* gotten test failures, particularly with top_p. It's because of the way these values work: they change the sampling data for the language models, so sometimes you get variable results. if you run these tests and get failures, it's not entirely unexpected, just like a test of a random number generator *should* give you an equal distribution of results but occasionally the universe just says, "no, you're getting similar numbers back for a while." Getting that kind of result **consistently** is bad, but it *does* happen.

CHAPTER 2   GETTING STARTED

Conversations and Roles

What we've seen so far is a fairly simple query mechanism, a rough analogy to a single query to a given LLM, although we've given ourselves a way to control how variable a given response might be. That's useful, but not very; it means that every query exists in a sort of standalone universe.[9]

Given that LLMs are presented as conversational, it's time for us to see how that works and how we can manage a conversation with Spring AI.

We've used a *very* simple `Prompt` object, one accepting a `String` (and, perhaps, a `ChatOptions` object). This is *useful* but very *simple*—too simple, really, except for simple uses as we've shown so far.

What new `Prompt("When was Churchill in office")` does is relatively simple, but very instructive: that particular constructor delegates to a *different* constructor, that accepts a `UserMessage` with the contents of that string.

So what, then, is a `UserMessage`? It's a message from, of all things, a user. This implies that there are other types of messages, and there certainly are. They're actually rather important, in various ways, for building a conversation with an LLM.

There are three main types of messages in the LLM space right now: one is `user`. Another is `assistant`, and the third is `system`.

We actually have seen `assistant` messages already; that's the role assigned to messages *from the LLM*. Therefore, when we ask an LLM "What is the definition of a Chinese junk?", that query is sent as conversation with that element being from the `user` role, and the answer comes back as a message from the `assistant` role.

We can actually build a series of messages as our prompt, assigning the appropriate roles as we like, using `UserMessage` and establishing context with `AssistantMessage` instances from the system.

---

[9] Our "variability tests" with `temperature` relied on each query being standalone.

CHAPTER 2 GETTING STARTED

The first thing we need to do is to create a service that accepts a List of messages, because our other services are geared around simple queries with one input only. Thankfully, this is entirely supported by Prompt, which has a constructor that accepts List<Message>; our new UpdateChatService will do little more than handle the plumbing of constructing the actual Prompt and returning the response.

Listing 2-16. chapter02/src/main/java/ch02/service/ConversationChatService.java

```java
package ch02.service;

import org.springframework.ai.chat.client.ChatClient;
import org.springframework.ai.chat.messages.Message;
import org.springframework.ai.chat.model.Generation;
import org.springframework.ai.chat.prompt.Prompt;
import org.springframework.ai.openai.OpenAiChatOptions;
import org.springframework.stereotype.Service;

import java.util.List;

@Service
public class ConversationChatService extends OptionChatService {
    ConversationChatService(ChatClient.Builder builder) {
        super(builder);
    }

    public List<Generation> converse(List<Message> messages) {
        return converse(messages, new OpenAiChatOptions.
            Builder().build());
    }
```

CHAPTER 2   GETTING STARTED

```java
    public List<Generation> converse(
            List<Message> messages,
            OpenAiChatOptions options
    ) {
        var prompt = new Prompt(messages, options);
        return client.prompt(prompt).call().chatResponse().
        getResults();
    }
}
```

The test class for this is a little larger than some of our other classes so far. Let's take a look.

Listing 2-17. chapter02/src/test/java/ ch02/ConversationTests.java

```java
package ch02;

import ch02.service.ConversationChatService;
import org.apache.commons.text.WordUtils;
import org.junit.jupiter.api.*;
import org.slf4j.Logger;
import org.slf4j.LoggerFactory;
import org.springframework.ai.chat.messages.AssistantMessage;
import org.springframework.ai.chat.messages.Message;
import org.springframework.ai.chat.messages.UserMessage;
import org.springframework.ai.chat.model.Generation;
import org.springframework.beans.factory.annotation.Autowired;
import org.springframework.boot.test.context.SpringBootTest;

import java.util.ArrayList;
import java.util.List;

import static org.junit.jupiter.api.Assertions.assertTrue;
```

CHAPTER 2 GETTING STARTED

```
@SpringBootTest(webEnvironment = SpringBootTest.
WebEnvironment.MOCK)
@TestMethodOrder(MethodOrderer.OrderAnnotation.class)
public class ConversationTests {
    private final Logger log = LoggerFactory.getLogger(this.
    getClass());
    @Autowired
    ConversationChatService conversationChatService;

    /**
     * This method extracts the `AssistantMessage` from the
     generated LLM output
     * @param output the results of the call to the LLM
     * @return the first `AssistantMessage` in the output
     */
    private AssistantMessage getAssistantMessage(List
    <Generation> output) {
        return output.getFirst().getOutput();
    }

    /**
     * This method simply wraps the content and dumps it to
     a logger.
     * @param content A string to display
     */
    private void display(String content) {
        var lines = WordUtils
                .wrap(content, 62, "\n", true)
                .split("\\n");
        for (String line : lines) {
            log.info(line);
        }
```

```java
        log.info("-----");
    }

    @Test
    @Order(1)
    void simpleConversation() {
        var conversation = conversationChatService.
        converse(List.of(
                new UserMessage("What is the slope of y=x*1.2/z
                if z=2?")
        ));
        var output = getAssistantMessage(conversation);

        display(output.getContent());
        assertTrue(output.getContent().contains("0.6"));
    }

    @Test
    @Order(2)
    void interactiveConversation() {
        // we want to make a mutable list, because we're adding
        context.
        List<Message> messages = new ArrayList<>();
        messages.add(
                new UserMessage("What is the slope of y=x*1.2/z
                if z=2?")
        );
        var conversation = conversationChatService.
        converse(messages);
        var output = getAssistantMessage(conversation);

        display(output.getContent());
        assertTrue(output.getContent().contains("0.6"));
```

```
        // we want to establish the context of the
        first answer.
        messages.add(output);

        // now we want to add some extra context of our own...
        messages.add(
                new UserMessage("And if z=3?")
        );
        conversation = conversationChatService.
        converse(messages);
        output = getAssistantMessage(conversation);
        display(output.getContent());

        assertTrue(output.getContent().contains("0.4"));
    }
}
```

The first part of the test has some utility methods that we'll want: one is a convenience method to help us extract the `AssistantMessage` returned by the API, and the other is a display method to dump wrapped output to a logger. Neither one is *necessary*, but they're handy to have around.

Next we have `simpleConversation()`, a test method that validates that `ConversationChatService` is able to replicate the functionality we expect our services to have: can we ask an LLM a simple question? We're pretending to be math-challenged for this test, because that gives us a concrete answer we can look for; if our output doesn't have *the actual answer to our question*, we want to fail the test.

The real test is `interactiveConversation()`. This method has a lot of bits in it, so let's deconstruct it.

The first part of `interactiveConversation()` replicates `simpleConversation()`; the main difference is that it constructs a `List<Message>` and uses that with the `UpdateChatService`, instead of constructing an immutable `List` in place. We also preserve the `AssistantMessage`.

After we validate (and display) the output, we add the AssistantMessage to the messages. Thus, it's a List with two entries: a UserMessage (our original query) and an AssistantMessage that has the LLM explaining the slope of our equation. We then **refine our query** by changing a parameter, but with a question that has no context in and of itself: we alter the value of z with another UserMessage.

Consider what is happening here: we're asking And if z=3? with nothing else; if you walked up to a mathematician—or asked an LLM—that simple question, out of the blue, they'd rationally ask you for more context.

In fact, we did exactly that with ChatGPT:

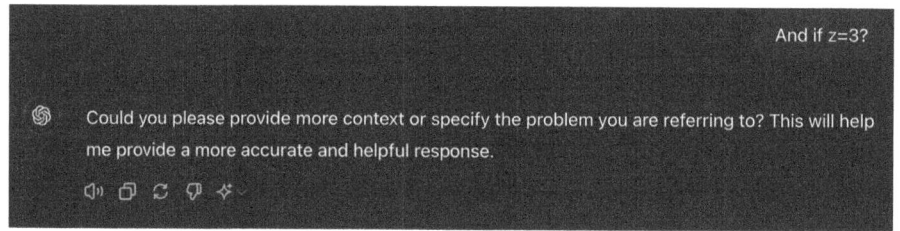

Asking a math question without context

So now we have a valid way to test: by appending And if z=3? as a UserMessage with the prior context of our initial question and the LLM's response, we can see if it factors in the conversation.

Note This is not a perfect test. Ideally, we'd have the LLM infer something *not in our question* and use that for future context in the conversation. Given that we all understand this, why doesn't our test apply context from the LLM as well? The answer is simple: "Because it's much harder to test." Our series of questions here have objective answers, and having the LLM alter the context makes the answers *subjective*, and we really want to actually *test something* instead of displaying it and hoping it works out.

To actually make all this work, we simply add another `UserMessage` (with the text `And if z=3?`) to the list of messages, and create another interaction with the LLM. This gives the LLM a chance to examine the context of the question (including our first query and its original answer) and give us the revised response.

We can also use `SystemMessage` as part of the conversation. A *system message* is an edict for the LLM to factor in; it can be similar to a `UserMessage` in impact, but *in general* a system message is more likely to have a persistent impact over the entire conversation; a `UserMessage` might, for example, change the conversational mode to Diogenes instead, but a `SystemMessage` is harder for the user to override.

This is an interesting example—but we can take it further, and we will, in the next chapter. Our `ConversationTests` example shows context as part of the conversation, but our test looks for a very simple answer—"does the result contain this bit of text that represents what we expect?" and we can do better. It's one of the more compelling features of Spring AI, and we're going to look at it in our next chapter, where we discuss concrete data extraction.

Next Steps

In our next chapter, we're going to look at Spring AI's output converters, where we can get the LLM to give us structured data for our program to consume directly, along with some mechanisms for allowing the AI to gather data from our programs.

CHAPTER 3

Asking Questions and Using Data

In our last chapter, we explored setting up our project and querying an LLM. In this chapter, we're going to explore two other important aspects of the LLM infrastructure—getting structured data out of them and feeding data **to** an LLM on demand by way of providing functions.

It may seem odd to think about providing access points to an AI, but this is a crucial lever for applying what the LLMs can do for you.

Interacting with an AI

For the most part, AIs consist of data and a reasoning process about that data. The model tends to be fairly static, as creating a model is expensive in terms of resources, and models tend to be focused on spheres of knowledge. Most of the popular models, like `gpt4-o` (one of the commercial models from ChatGPT), are huge and focused on generalized knowledge; they might be good for the questions you ask, or they might not. Other models, like Github's Copilot or the Qwen models, are designed for coding, and some are finely tuned for specific programming languages.

CHAPTER 3   ASKING QUESTIONS AND USING DATA

The key feature of all of these, however, is that they **were trained**—note the past tense. Most of them provide information about when they were trained, to give some context to what they know, and many of them will also answer time-sensitive questions about current events by informing you that their training data didn't include recent history.

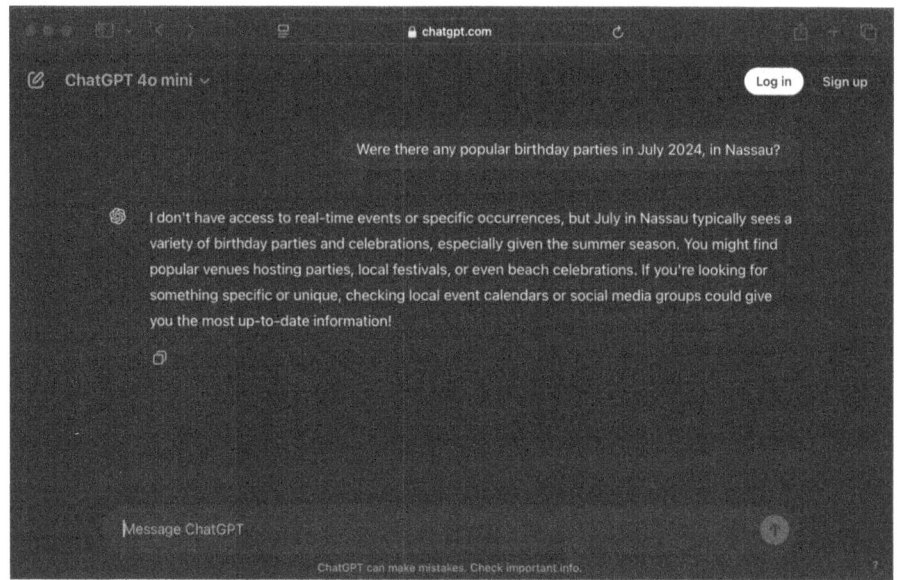

Asking an LLM about current events

The LLM isn't *wrong*—checking local calendars or social media isn't a bad strategy!—but it limits the AI to being a useful but fairly passive research tool.[1]

The problem, then, lies in how to provide access of, well, *something*, to the LLM. It's not just *data* or *current events*, it's a matter of providing interactions to the LLM, such that it can find out something that its knowledge model does not have or provide functionality that it *shouldn't have*.

---

[1] What's more, given the nature of how LLMs work, even as a research tool, it requires verification, about which most responsible LLMs will explicitly remind you.

This is how one might be able to use ChatGPT as it is **today** to query order status or perhaps even **make** an order.

Working with the "Real World"

We can build a working example of something you might find in the real world by thinking of smart lights. There are many commercial examples of smart lightbulbs on the market today, and one can work with them in multiple ways, whether with Alexa, Nest, the custom apps associated with each brand, or home controller applications like openHAB[2] or Home Assistant.[3]

We're going to build something like openHAB: we're going to create a Spring service to control software "light bulbs," and then we'll provide ways to query and control them through interactions with OpenAI.

Note It would be fairly trivial to take our planned light bulb manager and migrate to work with **actual** light bulbs. This is something one of your authors did for a living. It's actually rather fun, but we're not going to assume our readers have a specific brand of smart lights[4] or that they want to annoy their wives by changing the lights through fooling around with software, either.

---

[2] openHAB can be found at https://www.openhab.org/.
[3] Home Assistant's home page is https://www.home-assistant.io/.
[4] The Matter API (https://developers.home.google.com/matter) actually helps synchronize a lot of smart device controls, but Matter's API requires a lot of investment, and that's out of the scope of this book. Apart from Matter, you're writing to a set of specific manufacturers' specifications, and that's difficult to generalize and often inconsistent, to boot. Our software emulations carry the day for simplicity and consistency and, well, cost.

CHAPTER 3 ASKING QUESTIONS AND USING DATA

With that said, let's get started. First, we need our directory structure and our `pom.xml`.

Listing 3-1. Creating the directory structure in a POSIX shell

```
# in a POSIX shell
mkdir -p chapter03/src/{main,test}/{java/ch03,resources}
```

The `pom.xml` is very straightforward. It could have been copied from Chapter 2 with few changes, but we actually have fewer dependencies in Chapter 3 than we did in Chapter 2.

Listing 3-2. chapter03/pom.xml

```xml
<?xml version="1.0" encoding="UTF-8"?>

<project xmlns="http://maven.apache.org/POM/4.0.0"
         xmlns:xsi="http://www.w3.org/2001/XMLSchema-instance"
         xsi:schemaLocation="http://maven.apache.org/POM/4.0.0
         http://maven.apache.org/xsd/maven-4.0.0.xsd">
    <modelVersion>4.0.0</modelVersion>
    <parent>
        <groupId>com.apress</groupId>
        <artifactId>bsai-code</artifactId>
        <version>1.0</version>
    </parent>

    <artifactId>chapter03</artifactId>
    <version>1.0</version>

    <dependencies>
        <dependency>
            <groupId>org.springframework.ai</groupId>
            <artifactId>spring-ai-openai-spring-boot-starter
            </artifactId>
        </dependency>
```

```xml
<dependency>
    <groupId>org.springframework.boot</groupId>
    <artifactId>spring-boot-starter-web</artifactId>
</dependency>
<dependency>
    <groupId>org.springframework.boot</groupId>
    <artifactId>spring-boot-starter-test</artifactId>
    <scope>test</scope>
    <exclusions>
        <exclusion>
            <groupId>com.vaadin.external.google
            </groupId>
            <artifactId>android-json</artifactId>
        </exclusion>
    </exclusions>
</dependency>
    </dependencies>
</project>
```

Now for the more interesting stuff: our lights. Our basic light abstraction is very simple (and not very accurate, from a real-world light modeling perspective): we have lights, identified by color, that have a state of being "on" or "off."

Note In the real world, smart bulbs have a number of identifying characteristics: IP Addresses, MAC addresses, names, and perhaps zones. They also have more mutable characteristics, **including** color (most of the time!), brightness, and color temperature, and they also can provide metrics for their use. However, none of these attributes help us model calling functions from Spring AI, so we're ignoring them.

The `Light` class is a model—it's a representation of a thing—so we're going to put it in the `ch03.model` package, in `chapter03/src/main/java/ch03/model/Light.java`. The code for it is very straightforward; it's a classic Plain Old Java Object (not a `record`) because we're going to mutate its state. Again, we're aiming for simplicity here.[5]

Listing 3-3. chapter03/src/main/java/ch03/model/Light.java

```java
package ch03.model;

import java.util.StringJoiner;

public class Light {
    private String color;
    private Boolean on;

    public Light(String color, boolean on) {
        this.color = color;
        this.on = on;
    }

    // included for serialization later
    public Light() {
    }

    public String getColor() {
        return color;
    }
```

---

[5] We toyed with the idea of making an unimpeachably correct representation, including the use of `record` and other such things. We decided against it, because we're not trying to stun readers—or, well, **attempt** to stun readers—with how most excellent and FP-compliant our *simple example code* was. We just want it to work and be easy to understand.

```java
    public void setColor(String color) {
        this.color = color;
    }

    public boolean isOn() {
        return on;
    }

    public void setOn(boolean on) {
        this.on = on;
    }

    @Override
    public String toString() {
        return new StringJoiner(", ",
                Light.class.getSimpleName() + "[", "]")
                .add("color='" + color + "'")
                .add("on=" + on)
                .toString();
    }
}
```

The next thing we'll need to do is create a `LightService`—in `ch03.service`—that works with instances of our `Light` class. This is a Spring component, and the heart of its functionality is in the `getLights()` method, which queries the Spring `ApplicationContext` for any managed instances of `Light`.

In a real application, this class would have network services to track when lights became available or responded to network broadcast events, but the actual mechanics of that are **far** too complex for this example.

After we see the source for `LightService`, we're going to create our Spring configuration, and then we'll test all this stuff out so we know it works.

Listing 3-4. chapter03/src/main/java/ch03/service/LightService.java

```java
package ch03.service;

import ch03.model.Light;
import org.slf4j.Logger;
import org.slf4j.LoggerFactory;
import org.springframework.context.ApplicationContext;
import org.springframework.stereotype.Service;

import java.util.List;
import java.util.Optional;

@Service
public class LightService {
    public final Logger logger = LoggerFactory.getLogger(this.getClass());

    ApplicationContext context;

    public LightService(ApplicationContext context) {
        this.context = context;
    }

    public List<Light> getLights() {
        return context
                .getBeansOfType(Light.class)
                .values()
                .stream()
                .toList();
    }

    public Optional<Light> getLight(String color) {
        return getLights()
                .stream()
```

```
            .filter(light -> light.getColor().
            equalsIgnoreCase(color))
            .findFirst();
    }

    public Optional<Light> setLight(String color, boolean
    status) {
        var light = getLight(color);
        light.ifPresent(it -> {
            it.setOn(status);
        });
        return light;
    }
}
```

This service provides three methods: one is getLights(), which—as previously stated—gets all of the managed Light instances from Spring. The getBeansOfType() method returns a Map<String, Class<T>>—where the key is the name of the bean in the Spring context and the Class is the type passed in—and we don't care about the name of the beans, so we convert it to a simple List.

The next method provided retrieves a Light by color. If the color isn't found among the list of Light instances, an empty result is returned; this is a pattern largely inspired by the Spring Data Repository. We could have used nullable types instead, as Optional<T> references are nullable in and of themselves.[6]

---

[6] Optional is useful in Java, but not very; however, in streams they can occasionally be quite useful. We're not going to get anywhere near the tipping point where we see value from using Optional like that, but it's good to follow a convention, and this is one.

The last method provides a mechanism to change a light's state. It assumes the state passed in is absolute; it won't complain if you try to turn on a light that's already on, for example; nor will it complain if you change a light that doesn't exist. In this case, it simply returns an empty `Optional` just like `getLight()` does.

Like our `Light` class, the `LightService` isn't particularly complex or interesting; we just need to have it to make everything else work, much as we need our *next* class, the `Ch03Configuration` class, which is our Spring configuration.

This class exists mostly to give us a place for the `@SpringBootApplication` annotation as well as instantiate our `Light` instances. Thus, it's just as simple as `Light` and `LightService`:

Listing 3-5. chapter03/src/main/java/ch03//Ch03Configuration.java

```java
package ch03;

import ch03.model.Light;
import org.springframework.boot.autoconfigure.SpringBootApplication;
import org.springframework.context.annotation.Bean;

@SpringBootApplication
public class Ch03Configuration {
    @Bean
    Light getYellowLight() {
        return new Light("yellow", false);
    }

    @Bean
    Light getRedLight() {
        return new Light("red", false);
    }
```

```
    @Bean
    Light getGreenLight() {
        return new Light("green", false);
    }

    @Bean
    Light getBlueLight() {
        return new Light("blue", false);
    }
}
```

Note that there's no correlation of light colors to bean names. We could have named the beans "more appropriately," but again, in any kind of real-world analog, we'd not create light references in this manner; they'd be discovered, so this class is entirely used for building out our examples, which we're quite aware haven't even *begun* to touch Spring AI.

Spring AI integration is coming, we promise. We're almost there: we just need a test to validate that our `LightService` and the configuration is doing what it's supposed to, and that involves two *more* classes—one of which is a base class for our tests that provides common services.

Let's look at our `BaseLightTests` class first; it's a test class, so it goes in chapter03/src/test/java/ch03. It provides a common reference to a `LightService` (so our tests don't have to include one), as well as methods to reset all available lights to being "off"—so we have a pristine test state every time—and assert that a light exists and has a given state, as well as a method to construct a map of lights to their status, which means it's easier for us to test the state of **all** lights.

Chapter 3　Asking Questions and Using Data

Listing 3-6.　chapter03/src/test/java/ch03/BaseLightTests.java

```java
package ch03;

import ch03.model.Light;
import ch03.service.LightService;
import org.junit.jupiter.api.BeforeEach;
import org.slf4j.Logger;
import org.slf4j.LoggerFactory;
import org.springframework.beans.factory.annotation.Autowired;
import org.springframework.boot.test.context.SpringBootTest;

import java.util.List;
import java.util.Map;
import java.util.stream.Collectors;

import static org.junit.jupiter.api.Assertions.assertEquals;
import static org.junit.jupiter.api.Assertions.assertTrue;

@SpringBootTest
public abstract class BaseLightTests {
    private final Logger logger = LoggerFactory.getLogger
    (this.getClass());
    @Autowired
    LightService lightService;

    @BeforeEach
    void turnAllLightsOff() {
        lightService
                .getLights()
                .forEach(light -> {
                    light.setOn(false);
                });
    }
```

```
    final void assertState(String color, boolean on) {
        var light = lightService.getLight(color);
        assertTrue(light.isPresent(), color + " light is
        present");
        assertEquals(on, light.get().isOn(), "light state");
    }

    final Map<String, Boolean> mapToStatus(List<Light>
    response) {
        return response
                .stream()
                .collect(
                        Collectors.toMap(Light::getColor,
                        Light::isOn)
                );
    }
}
```

Now it's finally time for us to round out our simple example of light services, with a test of the, well, LightService. This class extends BaseLightTests so it gets a reference to the LightService, and every test it has will start with all lights being set to *off*.

Listing 3-7. chapter03/src/test/java/ch03/LightServiceTests.java

package ch03;

import ch03.service.LightService;
import org.junit.jupiter.api.Test;
import org.springframework.beans.factory.annotation.Autowired;
import org.springframework.boot.test.context.SpringBootTest;

import static org.junit.jupiter.api.Assertions.*;

```java
@SpringBootTest
public class LightServiceTests extends BaseLightTests {
    @Autowired
    LightService lightService;

    @Test
    void testLights() {
        // we expect four lights in our configuration.
        assertEquals(4, lightService.getLights().size(), "count
        of lights");
    }

    @Test
    void findLight() {
        // we need to be able to find a specific light.
        assertTrue(lightService.getLight("yellow").
        isPresent());
    }

    @Test
    void failToFindMissingLight() {
        // we need to be able to make sure a light
        doesn't exist.
        assertTrue(lightService.getLight("purple").isEmpty());
    }

    @Test
    void changeLight() {
        assertState("yellow", false);
        // set the light on
        lightService.setLight("yellow", true);
        assertState("yellow", true);
```

```
        // turn it back off, restoring original state
        lightService.setLight("yellow", false);
        assertState("yellow", false);
    }
}
```

The code here is remarkably simple, as is the rest of our code: we know what our configuration should be (four lights, and "purple" should not be among them), and we simply run through all of our `LightService` methods to make sure they return values we expect.

We're not really being exhaustive here, but we're being exhaustive *enough* for our example code. If this test passes completely, we have quite a bit of confidence that our `LightService` is functional in the ways we expect it to be.

It's finally time for us to look at *using* this from Spring AI.

Providing Access to Your Data

The core concept here is that we're providing a way for the AI to do two things: determine *when* we're referring to something our code controls and providing access to whatever it is.

If the data is static, we could always provide it to the AI as part of the request. For example, if we wanted a summary of a web page, we might fetch the web page's content (with JSoup[7] or something like it) and provide that as part of the request.

---

[7] JSoup (`https://jsoup.org/`) is a Java library that makes extraction of data from HTML or XML very trivial: many HTML and XML documents are poorly formed, and JSoup is quite permissive in how it parses.

Listing 3-8. An example AI request for content summary

```
I have a web page with the following content, for which
I'd like a summary and any interesting observations about
the author:

```

This is My About Page

My name is Lorem Ipsum. I like hamsters and most other small
mammals, like squirrels and rabbits. I'm pretty indiscriminate
in which mammals I like; rodents, lagomorphs, procyonids,
they're all wonderful
creatures.

I like gnawing on tree stumps, too. I may have had a didelphoid
in my family tree at some point.
```

---

**Note** You should feel free to use this as a prompt for any GPT you prefer; it's not likely to tell you much you didn't already know, though. To really get anything out of it, you'd want a much larger body of input.

---

This approach works if you know what information you intend to provide to the language model. In this case, you're focusing its attention specifically on the plain-text content of a web page (presumably; we made that content up as we wrote), so there's no need for "live access" to the data.

You could also provide a table of information, corresponding to the lights we've set up in our Spring configuration in Listing 3-5.
```

Listing 3-9. An example AI request for finding the status of a light

```
Here's a CSV representation of a set of light bulbs.
Can you tell me the status of the lights named 'yellow' and
'purple'?

```
name,state
yellow,on
red,off
blue,off
green,off
```
```

This should result in the AI telling us that the light named `yellow` is "on" and that the state of the light named `purple` cannot be determined, as we didn't provide its data.

The issues with doing this are twofold: one issue is that the light data isn't "live"—what if someone changes the light after issuing the request?

Another issue is that we're providing far more data than our request actually needs. We only need to provide the data for the light named `yellow`, since that's the only *existing* light we have in our query, and the other lights are simply consuming tokens for the AI to parse. Token parsing isn't *expensive*, really, but imagine we were querying the lights for, say, a hospital, which might have *thousands* of such lights—parsing all of that data adds up to real money and time.

Let's do better.

Building the Callable for Spring AI

To provide functionality to Spring AI, we use a *named service* that has a description to help the AI determine whether the service can provide data or not. That service is an implementation of a `java.util.function.Function<T,R>`, that accepts a data element as a request and returns a

CHAPTER 3   ASKING QUESTIONS AND USING DATA

response. When we build our prompt, we will provide the name of our service as part of the prompt, and *in general* the LLMs do a good job of determining when and how to call the function.

Let's take a look at how this is done, first by replicating our query of the status of lights named yellow and purple. This won't compile until we have a few other classes written, but we're going to get to them in very short order.

Here's RequestLightStatusTest.java, which uses a service to talk to the AI. Again, *we haven't written that service* yet, but it's coming up very soon.

Listing 3-10. chapter03/src/test/java/ch03/RequestLightStatusTest.java

```java
package ch03;

import ch03.service.RequestChatService;
import org.junit.jupiter.api.Test;
import org.slf4j.Logger;
import org.slf4j.LoggerFactory;
import org.springframework.ai.chat.messages.UserMessage;
import org.springframework.beans.factory.annotation.Autowired;
import org.springframework.boot.test.context.SpringBootTest;

import java.util.List;

import static org.junit.jupiter.api.Assertions.assertTrue;

@SpringBootTest
public class RequestLightStatusTest extends BaseLightTests {
    Logger logger= LoggerFactory.getLogger(this.getClass());
    @Autowired
    RequestChatService lightQueryService;

    @Test
```

```
    void queryLightStatus() {
        var response = lightQueryService.converse(List.of(
                new UserMessage("Can you tell me the status of
                the lights named 'yellow' and 'purple'?")
        ));

        var content=response.getFirst().getOutput().
        getContent();

        logger.info("Response: {}", content);
        assertTrue(content.contains("off"));
    }
}
```

This test is, honestly, not very good: it replicates our query well enough, but the output is not tested very well.[8]

The test fails if the response doesn't contain the word "off"—which we expect it will, because that's the default state of the `yellow` light—but doesn't have a good way to validate that the `purple` light isn't present. Once we have the other classes required for this test built, we'll be able to see what the query responds with and validate it **that** way—and there are ways to do it programmatically, but we haven't covered those yet. We're getting there.

What we need next is a `RequestChatService`. It's going to look an awful lot like our `ConversationChatService` from Chapter 2, in Listing 2-16, but it's going to introduce a method to build our `OpenAiChatOptions` object that we'll use explicitly in calling the AI, `buildOptions()`.

---

[8] The difficulty of testing textual responses is going to come up later in this chapter and will also be addressed in Chapter 6.

CHAPTER 3   ASKING QUESTIONS AND USING DATA

This `OpenAiChatOptions` object will include a reference to a named service, `RequestLightStatusFunction`, that we'll see next—this is the named function that allows a light's status to be queried.

Listing 3-11. chapter03/src/main/java/ch03/service/RequestChatService.java

```java
package ch03.service;

import org.springframework.ai.chat.client.ChatClient;
import org.springframework.ai.chat.messages.Message;
import org.springframework.ai.chat.model.Generation;
import org.springframework.ai.chat.prompt.Prompt;
import org.springframework.ai.openai.OpenAiChatOptions;
import org.springframework.context.annotation.Primary;
import org.springframework.stereotype.Service;

import java.util.List;

@Primary
@Service
public class RequestChatService {
    protected final ChatClient client;

    RequestChatService(ChatClient.Builder builder) {
        client = builder.build();
    }

    public OpenAiChatOptions buildOptions() {
        return new OpenAiChatOptions
                .Builder()
                .withFunction("RequestLightStatusService")
                .build();
    }
```

```
    public List<Generation> converse(
            List<Message> messages
    ) {
        var prompt = new Prompt(messages, buildOptions());
        return client
                .prompt(prompt)
                .call()
                .chatResponse()
                .getResults();
    }
}
```

This is fairly straightforward, but note the use of `@Primary` for the class. This is because we're going to extend this class with an `UpdateChatService` (Listing 3-14), and since Spring will look for any Spring bean that can be assigned to a reference, we need to tell it that if there's a choice, use *this* class and not any other matching class. Ordinarily, you wouldn't need to worry about this sort of thing.

With that said, we have *finally* gotten to the point where we can write our function.

It's important to note that this is a Component—declared with `@Component` here, so Spring knows to manage it. It could be a `@Bean` in our configuration, or a `@Service`—it's not really a service, despite the name, but as it operates *on* data and uses another service, it seemed appropriate enough as a name.[9]

---

[9] Readers should definitely feel free to use their own conventions. The power of conventions is not that *you* use *ours*—it's that whatever convention you use works for *you*.

The next important thing about the declaration, before we get to the code itself, is the use of a *description*, done here with the `@Description` annotation. This provides information to the AI about what the function does and should be written to provide hints; here, `get light status` provides enough information.

> **Note** Writing the descriptions might be the most challenging aspect of writing functions for Spring AI. Directness and clarity seem to be the most consistent approaches; you may have to try a few options in your own functions, testing along the way, to get them tuned well. Oddly enough, this advice applies to generalized queries to an LLM, too. There's no replacement for experience.

We need three pieces here: our input structure, our output structure, and the function that maps our input to the output.[10]

We can put all three in the same source file and scope the inputs and outputs to our component, as `record` types; our class is a Spring bean, so it has access to all of the wiring that the Spring context provides. In our case, we're having Spring provide a reference to a `LightService`, from Listing 3-4.

Listing 3-12. chapter03/src/main/java/ch03/service/RequestLightStatusFunction.java

```
package ch03.service;

import org.slf4j.Logger;
import org.slf4j.LoggerFactory;
```

---

[10] Interestingly enough, that's one of the definitions of a function in mathematics: a function literally maps an input to an output, deterministically. This is also the heart of "Functional Programming," and a core aspect of how streams work, and we've now wandered far away from the point of *this* book.

CHAPTER 3   ASKING QUESTIONS AND USING DATA

```java
import org.springframework.context.annotation.Description;
import org.springframework.stereotype.Service;

import java.util.function.Function;

@Service("RequestLightStatusService")
@Description("Get light status")
public class RequestLightStatusFunction
        implements Function<RequestLightStatusFunction.Request,
        RequestLightStatusFunction.Response> {
    public final Logger logger = LoggerFactory.getLogger(this.
    getClass());
    LightService lightService;

    public RequestLightStatusFunction(LightService
    lightService) {
        this.lightService = lightService;
    }

    public record Request(String color) {
    }

    public record Response(String color, boolean on) {
    }

    public Response apply(Request request) {
        logger.info("Requesting status for light: {}",
        request);
        var light = lightService.getLight(request.color);
        return light
                .map(value -> new Response(request.color,
                value.isOn()))
                .orElse(null);
    }
}
```

CHAPTER 3   ASKING QUESTIONS AND USING DATA

Our class has single attribute, the `LightService`, that provides access to our lights "live." We provide this via constructor injection, although we could just as easily have used autowiring.

Next, we have a `RequestLightStatusService.Request` record—which has a single field, a light's name. This is what the AI should provide to our function as an input.

After that, we have a `RequestLightStatusService.Response`—which binds the light's color to its status. This is what we provide to the AI as output from our function call.

Lastly, we have the actual mapping function, the `apply()` method. This looks up the light from the `LightService` and maps the `Optional<Light>` into either a valid `RequestLightStatusService.Response` object (if it exists) or `null` if not.

Note   As usual, we have a lot of options for how to map the response, given an input. This is one of a few sensible possibilities. It's also the one that occurred to your author first, and by gum, it worked well enough. After all, it's just taking an input and generating an output for it.

Now we have enough code that we can run our `RequestLightStatusTest` and see its output. Here's example output from our machines for this test:

```
INFO  ch03.service.RequestLightStatusFunction --
Requesting status for light: Request[color=yellow]
INFO  ch03.service.RequestLightStatusFunction --
Requesting status for light: Request[color=purple]
INFO  ch03.RequestLightStatusTest --
Response: The status of the light named 'yellow' is off.
Unfortunately, I couldn't retrieve the status of the light
named 'purple'.
```

Because this is generated with an LLM, the output can vary from call to call, but your output should map pretty closely to what this example shows. Assuming everything has gone well, you can see that the system reported the yellow light correctly—it's off, by default, after all—and you can see from the logging output that the function was called twice, once for the `yellow` light and once for the `purple` light.

It's time to write another function, one that *changes* a light's status, and then we can look at perhaps some better ways than plain text to get data out of the AI.

Changing a Light

The pattern for writing a mutation operation isn't any different from the pattern for writing an access. We have an input format—a request—and a response of some sort, and a mapping function to go from one to the other. In this case, we have input that should add the desired light's state in addition to the light's name, and the response… well, the response can be anything, but it probably makes sense to return the new light's information.

So in essence, our `UpdateLightStatusFunction` is going to be *just* like our `RequestLightStatusFunction`, with a mutation of the light and a `Request` that includes the desired light's state. Let's see what it looks like.

Listing 3-13. chapter03/src/main/java/ch03/service/ UpdateLightStatusFunction.java

```
package ch03.service;

import org.slf4j.Logger;
import org.slf4j.LoggerFactory;
import org.springframework.context.annotation.Description;
import org.springframework.stereotype.Service;

import java.util.function.Function;
```

```
@Service("ChangeLightStatusService")
@Description("Change a light's state")
public class UpdateLightStatusFunction
        implements Function<UpdateLightStatusFunction.Request,
        UpdateLightStatusFunction.Response> {
    public final Logger logger = LoggerFactory.getLogger(this.
    getClass());
    LightService lightService;

    public UpdateLightStatusFunction(LightService
    lightService) {
        this.lightService = lightService;
    }

    public record Request(String color, boolean on) {
    }

    public record Response(String color, boolean on) {
    }

    public Response apply(Request request) {
        logger.info("Changing status for light: {}", request);
        var light=lightService.setLight(request.color,
        request.on);
        return light
                .map(value -> new Response(request.color,
                value.isOn()))
                .orElse(null);
    }
}
```

It's so similar to `RequestLightStatusFunction` that one could conceive of writing a class hierarchy to build the functionality—you'd use a generic type for the `Request` and have localized functionality to apply

CHAPTER 3   ASKING QUESTIONS AND USING DATA

the request (i.e., a do-nothing operation for `RequestLightStatusFunction` and a mutation operation for `UpdateLightStatusFunction`). It'd be trivial to write, really, but wouldn't really accomplish anything for our purposes here, besides creating a few more listings. In the end, it'd probably end up with *more* lines of code, by a few, thanks to Java being slightly verbose.[11]

However, now we have to build another test—and another service— to show the functionality. It's going to look *very* similar to our previous example, but that's all right; authors get paid by the word.[12]

In our previous example, we wrote the test first, then the service the test used, and then the function—here, we've already seen the function, so let's continue inverting the process and take a look at the service that uses the function.

Here, though, we're going to use inheritance, because the only difference between `RequestChatService` and `UpdateChatService` is the provision of the `UpdateLightStatusFunction` function to the chat options.[13]

---

[11] If we put the functions in our Spring Configuration as `@Bean` instances rather than in separate source files, we could probably save a few lines here and there, but then it'd get a lot harder to explain in this chapter.

[12] We actually don't get paid by the word, or by the page. In the days of pulp fiction, in the 1950s, authors *were* paid by the word, which is why so much pulp fiction used purple prose—authors wrote out everything they could, so they would get paid more by the publisher. Speaking personally, your author here thinks that's a great idea; can we go back to that, Publisher?

[13] This is why Listing 3-11 used `@Primary`, because otherwise any reference to `RequestChatService` would be able to be fulfilled by either `RequestChatService` or `UpdateChatService`, and we wanted to tell Spring to prefer `RequestChatService` where possible; if we need an `UpdateChatService`, we'd use that reference type instead.

83

Listing 3-14. chapter03/src/main/java/ch03/service/UpdateChatService.java

```java
package ch03.service;

import org.springframework.ai.chat.client.ChatClient;
import org.springframework.ai.openai.OpenAiChatOptions;
import org.springframework.stereotype.Service;

@Service
public class UpdateChatService extends RequestChatService {
    public UpdateChatService(ChatClient.Builder builder) {
        super(builder);
    }

    @Override
    public OpenAiChatOptions buildOptions() {
        return new OpenAiChatOptions
                .Builder()
                .withFunction("RequestLightStatusService")
                .withFunction("ChangeLightStatusService")
                .build();
    }
}
```

And now it's time to take a look at a query that actually changes the lights' status. It's going to look much like the `RequestLightStatusTest` but will actually verify the lights' status after showing the response from the AI. Here, we actually have a better way of validating that our mutation was performed; this is a better test than `RequestLightStatusTest` was.

CHAPTER 3 ASKING QUESTIONS AND USING DATA

Listing 3-15. chapter03/src/test/java/ch03/UpdateLightStatusTest.java

```java
package ch03;

import ch03.service.UpdateChatService;
import org.junit.jupiter.api.Test;
import org.slf4j.Logger;
import org.slf4j.LoggerFactory;
import org.springframework.ai.chat.messages.UserMessage;
import org.springframework.beans.factory.annotation.Autowired;
import org.springframework.boot.test.context.SpringBootTest;

import java.util.List;

@SpringBootTest
public class UpdateLightStatusTest extends BaseLightTests {
    private final Logger logger = LoggerFactory.getLogger(this.getClass());
    @Autowired
    UpdateChatService lightConversationService;

    @Test
    void changeLightStatus() {
        var response = lightConversationService.converse
        (List.of(
                new UserMessage("Turn the yellow light on. " +
                        "Then show the state of the red," +
                        " green, blue, purple, and yellow lights.")
        ));
        logger.info("Response from service: {}",
                response.getFirst().getOutput().getContent());
```

85

CHAPTER 3   ASKING QUESTIONS AND USING DATA

```
        assertState("yellow", true);
        assertState("red", false);
    }
}
```

Our tests will pass (which means the function worked), but the test *also* generates the following output as an example:

```
INFO  ch03.service.UpdateLightStatusFunction --
Changing status for light: Request[color=yellow, on=true]
INFO  ch03.service.RequestLightStatusFunction --
Requesting status for light: Request[color=red]
INFO  ch03.service.RequestLightStatusFunction --
Requesting status for light: Request[color=green]
INFO  ch03.service.RequestLightStatusFunction --
Requesting status for light: Request[color=blue]
INFO  ch03.service.RequestLightStatusFunction --
Requesting status for light: Request[color=purple]
INFO  ch03.service.RequestLightStatusFunction --
Requesting status for light: Request[color=yellow]
INFO  ch03.UpdateLightStatusTest --
Response from service: The yellow light is now turned on.

Here are the states of the lights:
- Red light: Off
- Green light: Off
- Blue light: Off
- Purple light: Not available
- Yellow light: On
```

You can see the flow: first, it determined that it needed to mutate the yellow light, so called `UpdateLightStatusFunction` with `yellow` and `true` to turn the light "on"—and then it iterated through the lights we specified ("red," "green," "blue," "purple," and "yellow") to query their state, and it informed us that purple wasn't available, as the function to get the light returned null.

Structured Output

Our last test did a good job of verifying that the lights were actually changed, by using a single service (the `LightService`) to do everything, including applying changes from the AI. It's worth noting, though, that we can get the AI to give us actual data structures, so we can blend information from our data as well as information from the AI.

One way to do this is to instruct the AI to literally return formatted data: you might issue a query such as `provide the status of the lights in JSON format, with no commentary and no explanation.`, as a short example. Then we could take the response and pipe it through a JSON parser like Jackson[14] and access the resulting data structures.

That's... one way to do it. We can actually instruct Spring AI to do the work for us, though. Let's build a test that does the same thing as `UpdateLightStatusTest`, except that it returns a list of lights—and adds the CIE 1931 color coordinate of the light, inferred from its state and name.

CIE 1931 is a mathematical model that "define the relationship between the visible spectrum and the visual sensation of specific colors by human color vision."[15] It represents the colors we can see with an "x", "y", and "z" coordinate—where "z" is often shown as "Y", but that's confusing

---

[14] Jackson is the library that provides the default JSON parser in Spring Boot.
[15] CIE 1931: https://en.wikipedia.org/wiki/CIE_1931_color_space, captured on September 27, 2024.

in a book where users might not be familiar with the systems in question—and it's very common in APIs that work with smart lights, although it's not very common for users to work with the coordinate system directly. It was formalized in 1931, if you can imagine that from its name.

There are multiple ways to map data from Spring AI into an object model, but the easiest way is to simply construct the `OpenAiChatOptions` such that we use the `entity()` method, with a type reference that Jackson can recognize. We can even embed the data structures in our service, although it makes referencing them a little more verbose in calling code (as we'll see in our test).

Let's take a look, though. The service looks quite similar to our other Spring AI services, but it has some important differences.

Listing 3-16. chapter03/src/main/java/ch03/service/UpdateStructuredChatService.java

```java
package ch03.service;

import org.springframework.ai.chat.client.ChatClient;
import org.springframework.ai.chat.messages.Message;
import org.springframework.ai.chat.messages.SystemMessage;
import org.springframework.ai.openai.OpenAiChatOptions;
import org.springframework.stereotype.Service;

import java.util.ArrayList;
import java.util.List;

@Service
public class UpdateStructuredChatService {
    private final ChatClient client;

    public record LightWithXYZ(String color, boolean on,
    Double x, Double y, Double z) {
    }
```

CHAPTER 3   ASKING QUESTIONS AND USING DATA

```java
public record LightWithXYZList(List<LightWithXYZ> lights) {
}

public UpdateStructuredChatService(ChatClient.Builder
builder) {
    client = builder.build();
}

public OpenAiChatOptions buildOptions() {
    return new OpenAiChatOptions
            .Builder()
            .withFunction("RequestLightStatusService")
            .withFunction("ChangeLightStatusService")
            .build();
}

public LightWithXYZList converse(List<Message> messages) {
    var localMessages = new ArrayList<Message>(messages);
    localMessages.addFirst(new SystemMessage(
            "Add the CIE 1931 color representation of each
            light if possible."));
    return client
            .prompt()
            .messages(localMessages)
            .options(buildOptions())
            .call()
            .entity(LightWithXYZList.class);
    }
}
```

89

Chapter 3 Asking Questions and Using Data

The first differences are the use of the `LightWithXYZ` and `LightWithXYZList` records. The `LightWithXYZ` is basically a copy of our `Light` with added CIE 1931 information. The `LightWithXYZList` is simply a way to specify a list of the lights trivially (to avoid building more complex type references and whatnot).

Our `buildOptions()` is exactly the same as our other options methods, providing mutation and access to our lights to the AI.

Our `converse()` method does some extra things, though.

First, it uses a **system** message to instruct the AI with additional context, outside of whatever prompt the user supplies. In this case, we're telling the system to add the CIE 1931 representation of the lights, if possible (derived from their names and presence, so if the light's not found, we won't get any CIE 1931 information from it).

Secondly—and here's where the actual work of specifying structured data comes in—it uses `.entity(LightWithXYZList.class)` as the last part of the Spring AI request. This is all we need to do to ask the AI to try to coerce the output into a Java data structure that we can use.

There are other ways to specify mappings, if we have a more complex interaction, but this is the beginning of all of it, and even those other interactions are essentially doing something very similar.

Of course, now that we've talked about it, we should show it working, with a test. Here's `UpdateLightStructuredTest`.

Listing 3-17. chapter03/src/test/java/ch03/UpdateLightStructuredTest.java

```
package ch03;

import ch03.service.UpdateStructuredChatService;
import org.junit.jupiter.api.Test;
import org.springframework.ai.chat.messages.UserMessage;
import org.springframework.beans.factory.annotation.Autowired;
```

```java
import org.springframework.boot.test.context.SpringBootTest;

import java.util.List;

import static org.junit.jupiter.api.Assertions.*;

@SpringBootTest
public class UpdateLightStructuredTest extends BaseLightTests {
    @Autowired
    UpdateStructuredChatService service;

    UpdateStructuredChatService.LightWithXYZ find(
            String color,
            List<UpdateStructuredChatService.LightWithXYZ>
            lights
    ) {
        return lights
                .stream()
                .filter(i -> i.color().equalsIgnoreCase(color))
                .findFirst()
                .orElseThrow();
    }

    @Test
    void changeLightStatus() {
        // we use the actual types here for clarity only.
        // var would have worked fine.
        UpdateStructuredChatService.LightWithXYZList response =
                service.converse(List.of(
                        new UserMessage("Turn the yellow
                        light on. " +
                                "Then show the state of the " +
                                "red, green, blue, purple, and
                                yellow lights.")
                ));
```

CHAPTER 3   ASKING QUESTIONS AND USING DATA

```
        UpdateStructuredChatService.LightWithXYZ yellow =
                find("yellow", response.lights());
        assertTrue(yellow.on());
        assertEquals(0.4447, yellow.x(), 0.01);
        assertEquals(0.5153, yellow.y(), 0.01);
        assertEquals(0.04, yellow.z(), 0.01);

        UpdateStructuredChatService.LightWithXYZ purple =
                find("purple", response.lights());
        assertNull(purple.x());
        assertNull(purple.y());
        assertNull(purple.z());
    }
}
```

We have much the same structure as our other tests, and our query is the same. We have a method to get a specific light from our data structure (because it's returned as an `ArrayList`), but our test takes the data structure, finds both `yellow` and `purple`, and validates their state **and** that their CIE colors are roughly correct.

You'll note the use of actual data types in the test method, like `UpdateLightStructuredTest.LightWithXYZList`. This is entirely intentional and is purely to make the data types obvious to the reader. There's absolutely no need to use the data type's names if you don't want to; `var yellow` would have worked just as well.[16]

---

[16] When this chapter was being written, `var yellow` was actually the declaration used, for example. With that said, we felt we wanted to make the types more obvious, since they were being pulled from a service *and* exposed to client code, where our other embedded types were limited to their use in internal communications.

Applying This in Your Code

It's fun to see how an artificial set of lights can be queried and updated through the use of Spring AI, but that's not very practical, unless you're working with lights. In practice, though, you could imagine providing access to customer orders, or shipping status, or insurance policy conditions and states, or anything else: an automobile repair shop might have a way to track work orders such that a customer can ask an AI how things are going, rather than interrupting a human.

Human interaction is important in a lot of ways, and shouldn't be prevented—you wouldn't want to *force* a customer to talk to an AI rather than a human—but simple interactions can go much more smoothly with an AI, if they can be fulfilled by an AI. Imagine calling an expensive and talented mechanic away from working on a complex piece of machinery, only to ask "Is it done yet?"—when an AI could look at the status of the work order instead and reply with "No, but it's being worked on right now!" That's a win for everyone: the customer, because they can get an answer immediately, and the shop, because the mechanic doesn't have to get interrupted for a simple question.

Next Steps

In this chapter, we've seen how to provide two-way interaction between Spring AI and our code, such that the AI isn't limited to what data exists in its training set only, and it can use our functions to change things in our application. We've gone from a simple "fortune-teller" model, where we ask questions and the AI passively responds, to a model in which we can let the AI change the world around us.

CHAPTER 3   ASKING QUESTIONS AND USING DATA

It wouldn't be a stretch to imagine how these functions could return order information, or modify orders, or create tickets, or any other system interaction our applications needed; this is how many OpenAI-driven chatbots work, after all.

We've also seen some of how we can get the AI to present data in a fashion that our programs can easily interpret and apply.

In our next chapter, we're going to jump from the realm of working with text, into working with audio, both interpreting audio files and generating them.

CHAPTER 4

Working with Audio

Generating and Processing Audio

Since the early 19th century, humans have expressed the idea of a mechanical device capable of speech in fiction, through authors like Jules Verne and later H.G. Wells. By the mid-20th century in fiction, we had moved from "Ulla, Ulla" to machines that were capable of talking back (text to speech) and understanding speech (transcription). Today, we are surrounded by mechanical devices that have made the vision of Roddenberry and others come to life whether prefaced with "Computer," "Siri," or "Alexa" the result is a device that understands the basics of what you ask it like requests for weather or a piece of music.

Today, we can reasonably speak something as futuristic as "Computer, write me a chapter on using Spring AI to generate and process audio," and what would be returned might just be a good first start.[1] Since we're still actually writing the text here, let's turn our attention toward what we can achieve using AI with the spoken word. One can imagine transcribing video or audio to written text as part of a service offering. Written text can be spoken aloud using this module for the vision-impaired and for those engaged in activities where reading isn't an option or as a response to commands in a system like Siri.

---

[1] As we mentioned in Chapter 1, unless we mention it, the text of this book was written by one of the human authors.

© Andrew Lombardi and Joseph Ottinger 2025
A. Lombardi and J. Ottinger, *Beginning Spring AI*, Apress Pocket Guides,
https://doi.org/10.1007/979-8-8688-1291-0_4

CHAPTER 4   WORKING WITH AUDIO

Spring AI has two avenues for working with audio. The first is transcribing text from a supplied audio file, and the second is generating an audio file with natural sounding speech. In both instances, the integration done today with Spring AI uses OpenAI. Hopefully in the near future, we'll see integrations with other providers like Elevenlabs or Google's Gemini.

In this chapter, we will walk through the two simple APIs for processing audio and text and real-world examples of how you can use both.

Let's dive in.

The AI Spoken Word

Text-to-speech technology has a long history, dating back to the 1960s when Bell Labs used an IBM 7094 computer to synthesize speech for "Daisy Bell," even influencing Arthur C. Clarke's depiction of HAL9000 in *2001: A Space Odyssey*.

Text-to-speech synthesis is a fascinating programming challenge because it demands bridging the gap between abstract language and human perception. The models must grapple with not just grammar, but also the nuances of pronunciation, intonation, and rhythm that make speech sound natural.

This shift toward AI-powered solutions brings a host of benefits. Programmers now have access to a wider range of voices, more natural-sounding speech, and simpler integration processes. Service providers handle the heavy lifting, freeing developers to focus on creative applications and pushing the boundaries of flexible models.

The first task we'll take on is to create our directory structure for this chapter. This can be created in the "project directory" as in previous chapters with the following command, if you're running a POSIX shell like bash or zsh.

CHAPTER 4   WORKING WITH AUDIO

Listing 4-1. Creating the project directory structure in POSIX

```
mkdir -p src/{main,test}/{java,resources}
```

This is *this chapter's* project file, and thus it's in a directory *under* the top-level directory, called chapter04, and the file is named pom.xml.

Listing 4-2. chapter04/pom.xml

```xml
<?xml version="1.0" encoding="UTF-8"?>
<project xmlns="http://maven.apache.org/POM/4.0.0"
         xmlns:xsi="http://www.w3.org/2001/XMLSchema-instance"
         xsi:schemaLocation="http://maven.apache.org/POM/4.0.0
         http://maven.apache.org/xsd/maven-4.0.0.xsd">
    <modelVersion>4.0.0</modelVersion>
    <parent>
        <groupId>com.apress</groupId>
        <artifactId>bsai-code</artifactId>
        <version>1.0</version>
    </parent>

    <artifactId>chapter04</artifactId>
    <version>1.0</version>

    <properties>
    </properties>

    <dependencies>
        <dependency>
            <groupId>org.springframework.ai</groupId>
            <artifactId>spring-ai-openai-spring-boot-starter
            </artifactId>
        </dependency>
```

```xml
<dependency>
    <groupId>org.springframework.boot</groupId>
    <artifactId>spring-boot-starter-web</artifactId>
</dependency>
<dependency>
    <groupId>org.springframework.boot</groupId>
    <artifactId>spring-boot-starter-test</artifactId>
    <scope>test</scope>
    <exclusions>
        <exclusion>
            <groupId>com.vaadin.external.google
            </groupId>
            <artifactId>android-json</artifactId>
        </exclusion>
    </exclusions>
</dependency>
</dependencies>
<build>
    <plugins>
        <plugin>
            <groupId>org.springframework.boot</groupId>
            <artifactId>spring-boot-maven-plugin
            </artifactId>
            <configuration>
                <skip>false</skip>
            </configuration>
            <executions>
                <execution>
                    <goals>
                        <goal>repackage</goal>
                    </goals>
```

```
            </execution>
          </executions>
        </plugin>
      </plugins>
    </build>
</project>
```

The first thing we need to handle as we did in previous chapters is the application configuration. Thanks to the magic of the library `spring-ai-spring-boot-autoconfigure` which has the code for auto configuration, it will pick up the configuration for working with audio in your application configuration. We need to make sure we've provided a value to `spring.ai.openai.api-key`.

Listing 4-3. chapter04/src/main/java/ch04/Ch04Configuration.java

```
package ch04;

import org.springframework.ai.chat.client.ChatClient;
import org.springframework.boot.SpringApplication;
import org.springframework.boot.autoconfigure.SpringBootApplication;
import org.springframework.context.ApplicationContext;
import org.springframework.context.annotation.Bean;
import org.springframework.context.annotation.Description;

@SpringBootApplication
public class Ch04Configuration {

    public static void main(String[] args) {
        SpringApplication.run(Ch04Configuration.class, args);
    }
}
```

CHAPTER 4   WORKING WITH AUDIO

An `OpenAiAudioApi` has three main request modules that it enables for working with audio. The first we'll work with is the `SpeechRequest` which may just be the text we want to create an audio file but can also accept several other options which we'll go over below. As with other modules in Spring AI, they can be controlled at the point of the request, in code, or from the application properties.

Property name	Description
`spring.ai.openai.api-key`	The API key to be used by the application. This isn't utilized by `OpenAiAudioApi`, but we'll continue with this convention here.
`spring.ai.openai.audio.speech.options.model`	The name of the model to use. `tts-1` and `tts-1-hd` are both available.
`spring.ai.openai.audio.speech.options.voice`	The voice to use for the TTS output. Available options are `alloy`, `echo`, `fable`, `onyx`, `nova`, and `shimmer`.
`spring.ai.openai.audio.speech.options.response-format`	The format of the audio output, supported formats are `mp3`, `opus`, `aac`, `flac`, `wav`, and `pcm`.
`spring.ai.openai.audio.speech.options.speed`	The speed of the voice synthesis between `0.0` and `1.0`.

For this chapter, we're going to focus on tests, but also we will have an opportunity to explore a real-world case where we can use the Spring AI Audio API with Spring MVC.

We need to at least provide the API key to our chapter's code, and we want the model to be as deterministic as possible for now, so here's our `application.properties`. This is all very test-centric, so we're

CHAPTER 4   WORKING WITH AUDIO

going to place it in chapter02/src/test/resources. Note the use of spring.config.import, which allows us to load our .env file's values for internal use.

Listing 4-4. chapter04/src/test/resources/application.properties

```
spring.config.import=file:../.env[.properties]
spring.ai.openai.api-key=${OPENAI_API_KEY}
```

Our first test case is going to be based on the Daisy Bell song[2] that we referenced at the beginning of the chapter. Our test is simple; we're going to pass the lyrics to the song "Daisy Bell" to service TextToSpeechService and call the processText method. We'll take the response and assert that it is non-null as the actual response would be tough to verify in a test. (However, as we'll demonstrate, we can save it to local storage, where you can play it yourself and hear whether the AI actually fulfilled our request.)

Listing 4-5. chapter04/src/test/java/ch04/SpeechTTSTest.java

```
package ch04;

import ch04.service.TextToSpeechService;
import org.junit.jupiter.api.Test;
import org.springframework.beans.factory.annotation.Autowired;
import org.springframework.boot.test.context.SpringBootTest;

import static org.junit.jupiter.api.Assertions.assertNotNull;

@SpringBootTest(webEnvironment = SpringBootTest.WebEnvironment.MOCK)
public class SpeechTTSTest {
```

---

[2] As mentioned in the rather informative article, "The IBM 7094 is the First Computer to Sing," at https://www.historyofinformation.com/detail.php?entryid=4445—well worth reading.

```
    @Autowired
    TextToSpeechService textToSpeechService;

    @Test
    void runTTSQuery() {
        var responseAsBytes = textToSpeechService.
        processText("""
Daisy, Daisy,
Give me your answer, do!
I'm half crazy,
All for the love of you!
It won't be a stylish marriage,
I can't afford a carriage,
But you'll look sweet upon the seat
Of a bicycle built for two!
""", null);

        assertNotNull(responseAsBytes);
    }
}
```

If you are interested in the output as part of the test, you could write the mp3 to disk.

Listing 4-6. Write MP3 to disk

```
Files.write(Paths.get("./daisybell.mp3"), responseAsBytes);
```

This test is simple enough, but it obviously won't run because we don't have an implementation of the `TextToSpeechService` yet. The service has a single public method in it, `processText(String, OpenAiAudioSpeechOptions.Builder)`, which returns a `byte[]`.

We have a `SpeechModel` available which we'll use Spring's dependency injection to reference in our `TextToSpeechService`.

CHAPTER 4 WORKING WITH AUDIO

Issuing a call to OpenAI, we build a `SpeechPrompt` and pass the text we'd like to use to generate spoken word output. If we don't pass an `OpenAiAudioSpeechOptions` object into the `processText` method, it will by default use the options from `application.properties` if they're specified.

Once we have a prompt, we issue a call to the API, whether blocking or streaming; in this case, we don't care about streaming, so we use `call()` to get the response specification.

Once we have the response specification, we can get the recording by using the `getResult().getOutput()` method which returns a byte array. If we wanted to, we could get metadata about the call like the number of tokens consumed on our API key and a few other interesting elements.

This sounds pretty straightforward, so let's see what the actual Java class looks like.

Listing 4-7. chapter04/src/main/java/ch04/service/TextToSpeechService.java

```java
package ch04.service;

import org.springframework.ai.openai.OpenAiAudioSpeechModel;
import org.springframework.ai.openai.OpenAiAudioSpeechOptions;
import org.springframework.ai.openai.audio.speech.SpeechPrompt;
import org.springframework.ai.openai.audio.speech.SpeechResponse;
import org.springframework.stereotype.Service;

@Service
public class TextToSpeechService {

    private final OpenAiAudioSpeechModel speechModel;

    public TextToSpeechService(OpenAiAudioSpeechModel speechModel) {
        this.speechModel = speechModel;
    }
```

```
    public byte[] processText(String text,
    OpenAiAudioSpeechOptions.Builder speechOptions) {
        var speechPrompt = speechOptions != null ? new
        SpeechPrompt(text, speechOptions.build()) : new
        SpeechPrompt(text);
        SpeechResponse response = speechModel.call
        (speechPrompt);
        return response.getResult().getOutput();
    }
}
```

We've got something to test now, so we can run this chapter's test suite by using Maven:

```
mvn -am -pl chapter04 clean test
```

If everything is working properly, it should complete with SUCCESS. We've included what you should see in your output after running this command below.

```
[INFO] ------------------------------------------------------
[INFO]  T E S T S
[INFO] ------------------------------------------------------
[INFO] Running ch04.SpeechTTSTest
INFO  org.springframework.test.context.support.
AnnotationConfigContextLoaderUtils -- Could not detect default
configuration classes for test class [ch04.SpeechTTSTest]:
SpeechTTSTest does not declare any static, non-private, non-
final, nested classes annotated with @Configuration.
INFO  org.springframework.boot.test.context.SpringBootTest
ContextBootstrapper -- Found @SpringBootConfiguration ch04.
Ch04Configuration for test class ch04.SpeechTTSTest
[INFO] Tests run: 1, Failures: 0, Errors: 0, Skipped: 0, Time
elapsed: 2.532 s -- in ch04.SpeechTTSTest
```

CHAPTER 4   WORKING WITH AUDIO

If you chose to add the line for writing the file output to disk, you can open up the resulting MP3 file and have a listen. This test will sound more like spoken word than singing as there is no "singing" option within the OpenAI API; the result is a particularly passionless rendering of a silly love song and might be worth listening to only for humor's sake.

Let's say we wanted to pass some extra options to make it more like a song. Our endless testing with the API brought us to use the voice "Shimmer" and slow down the speed to 0.7 which makes it sound more like singing. We can pass a custom `OpenAiAudioSpeechOptions` with these options using a custom test like so.

Listing 4-8. chapter04/src/test/java/ch04/SpeechTTSTestWithOptions.java

```
package ch04;

import ch04.service.TextToSpeechService;
import org.junit.jupiter.api.Test;
import org.springframework.ai.openai.OpenAiAudioSpeechOptions;
import org.springframework.ai.openai.api.OpenAiAudioApi;
import org.springframework.beans.factory.annotation.Autowired;
import org.springframework.boot.test.context.SpringBootTest;

import java.io.IOException;
import java.nio.file.Files;
import java.nio.file.Paths;

import static org.junit.jupiter.api.Assertions.assertNotNull;

@SpringBootTest(webEnvironment = SpringBootTest.WebEnvironment.MOCK)
public class SpeechTTSTestWithOptions {

    @Autowired
    TextToSpeechService textToSpeechService;
```

```
    @Test
    void runTTSQuery() throws IOException {
        var responseAsBytes = textToSpeechService.
        processText("""
Daisy, Daisy,
Give me your answer, do!
I'm half crazy,
All for the love of you!
It won't be a stylish marriage,
I can't afford a carriage,
But you'll look sweet upon the seat
Of a bicycle built for two!
""", new OpenAiAudioSpeechOptions.Builder()
                .withModel(OpenAiAudioApi.TtsModel.TTS_1_HD.value)
                .withVoice(OpenAiAudioApi.SpeechRequest.Voice.
                SHIMMER)
                .withSpeed(0.7f)
        );

        Files.write(Paths.get("./daisybell.mp3"),
        responseAsBytes);

        assertNotNull(responseAsBytes);
    }

}
```

This test generates an MP3 file on disk which, with the given options, aims to sound more like a song. However, it's safe to say that vocalists like Celine Dion, Adele, and Janis Joplin have nothing to worry about from OpenAI just yet. The Whisper model we are using has been trained on the spoken word in the various supported languages. In order to provide

CHAPTER 4   WORKING WITH AUDIO

a method of "text-to-sing," we'd need to model the aspects of melody, pitch, rhythm, and the various other musical elements involved in realistic sounding singing.

There are general purpose TTS systems on the market today (Tacotron 2, WaveNet, and FastSpeech) that can be adapted by training the model on singing data including the music and patterns involved. It would also be important to provide the actual melody in the form of perhaps a MIDI file to teach the model the song it's singing.

Transcription

The other primary method available in these modules is the ability of Spring AI to integrate with a provider like OpenAI to transcribe audio of spoken words to text. Our tests previously have been using the lyrics to "Daisy Bell," and we will continue that here. A search on Wikipedia gives us a FLAC file of the original recording. If you'd like to download the file using the command line tool `curl`, you can see how to do that below, or opening a browser and saving the file to disk from the URL: https://bit.ly/daisy_bell_dectalk.

Listing 4-9. Download the Daisy Bell FLAC file

```
curl -O 'https://bit.ly/daisy_bell_dectalk'
```

Our transcription test will be based on this song; after downloading, you can place the file in the chapter's `src/test/resources` directory. The test is fairly simple, we'll read the file from the classpath and pass the audio content to the `TranscribeService` and call the single method `transcribeAudio`. The response we receive back will be verified using an assertion of a phrase from the original lyrics, because transcription is not an exact art. Even when the words match (as they usually will), the punctuation can be different, so an exact match of the output is unlikely. As a result, we're going to search for a phrase we do indeed fully expect to be in the output (the closing line) and leave it at that.

CHAPTER 4　WORKING WITH AUDIO

Let's take a look at our test.

Listing 4-10. chapter04/src/test/java/ch04/TranscribeTest.java

```
package ch04;

import ch04.service.TranscribeService;
import org.junit.jupiter.api.Test;
import org.springframework.ai.audio.transcription.AudioTranscriptionResponse;
import org.springframework.beans.factory.annotation.Autowired;
import org.springframework.boot.test.context.SpringBootTest;
import org.springframework.core.io.ClassPathResource;
import org.springframework.core.io.Resource;

import static org.junit.jupiter.api.Assertions.assertEquals;
import static org.junit.jupiter.api.Assertions.assertTrue;

@SpringBootTest(webEnvironment = SpringBootTest.WebEnvironment.MOCK)
public class TranscribeTest {

    @Autowired
    TranscribeService transcribeService;

    @Test
    void transcribeQuery() {
        Resource daisyBellResource = new
        ClassPathResource("Daisy_Bell_sung_by_DECtalk.flac");
        AudioTranscriptionResponse response = transcribeService
            .transcribeAudio(daisyBellResource, null);
        System.out.println(response.getResult().getOutput());
        assertTrue(response.getResult().getOutput().
        contains("the seat of a bicycle built for two"));
    }
}
```

CHAPTER 4　WORKING WITH AUDIO

We can't quite run this yet since the `TranscribeService` doesn't exist. If a reader looks at the assertion, we might also notice that what we're verifying is not exactly the original lyrics. Listening to the recording, we could definitely see how OpenAI would mistake "do" with "too." Now let's take a look at the `TranscribeService` and see how we make the transcription magic happen.

Listing 4-11. chapter04/src/main/java/ch04/service/TranscribeService.java

```java
package ch04.service;

import org.springframework.ai.audio.transcription.AudioTranscriptionPrompt;
import org.springframework.ai.audio.transcription.AudioTranscriptionResponse;
import org.springframework.ai.openai.OpenAiAudioTranscriptionModel;
import org.springframework.ai.openai.OpenAiAudioTranscriptionOptions;
import org.springframework.core.io.Resource;
import org.springframework.stereotype.Service;

@Service
public class TranscribeService {

    private final OpenAiAudioTranscriptionModel transcriptionModel;

    public TranscribeService(OpenAiAudioTranscriptionModel transcriptionModel) {
        this.transcriptionModel = transcriptionModel;
    }
```

```
    public AudioTranscriptionResponse transcribeAudio(Resource
    audioResource, OpenAiAudioTranscriptionOptions.Builder
    transcriptionOptions) {
        var transcriptionRequest = transcriptionOptions !=
        null ? new AudioTranscriptionPrompt(audioResource,
        transcriptionOptions.build()) : new AudioTranscriptionP
        rompt(audioResource);
        return transcriptionModel.call(transcriptionRequest);
    }
}
```

We have an `OpenAiAudioTranscriptionModel` available which we'll use Spring's dependency injection to reference in our `TranscribeService`.

Issuing a call to OpenAI, we build an `AudioTranscriptionPrompt` and pass the text we'd like to use to generate the output. If we don't pass an `OpenAiAudioTranscriptionOptions` object into the `transcribeAudio` method, it will by default use the options from `application.properties` if specified.

Once we have a prompt, we issue a call to the API, whether blocking or streaming; in this case, we don't care about streaming, so we use `call()` to get the response specification.

Once we have the response specification, we can get the recording by using the `getResult().getOutput()` method which returns a String. As with other calls, we could choose to look at the metadata which is available from the call to `getResult()` and for our test and usage we're focused only on the output.

We've got something to test now, so we can run this chapter's test suite by using Maven.

```
mvn -am -pl chapter04 clean test
```

CHAPTER 4 WORKING WITH AUDIO

If the stars align and the AI hasn't done any hallucinating during your test, you should see SUCCESS in the test. You can see a run for the TranscribeTest below.

```
[INFO] -------------------------------------------------------
[INFO] T E S T S
[INFO] -------------------------------------------------------
[INFO] Running ch04.TranscribeTest
INFO  org.springframework.test.context.support.
AnnotationConfigContextLoaderUtils -- Could not detect default
configuration classes for test class [ch04.TranscribeTest]:
TranscribeTest does not declare any static, non-private,
non-final, nested classes annotated with @Configuration.
INFO  org.springframework.boot.test.context.
SpringBootTestContextBootstrapper -- Found
@SpringBootConfiguration ch04.Ch04Configuration for test class
ch04.TranscribeTest

Powered by Spring Boot 3.3.0
INFO  ch04.TranscribeTest -- Starting TranscribeTest using Java
21.0.3 with PID 12317 (started by kinabalu in /Users/kinabalu/
workspace/beginningspring/bsai/code/chapter04)
INFO  ch04.TranscribeTest -- No active profile set, falling
back to 1 default profile: "default"
INFO  ch04.TranscribeTest -- Started TranscribeTest in 0.816
seconds (process running for 1.303)
WARNING: A Java agent has been loaded dynamically (/Users/
kinabalu/.m2/repository/net/bytebuddy/byte-buddy-agent/1.14.16/
byte-buddy-agent-1.14.16.jar)
WARNING: If a serviceability tool is in use, please run
with -XX:+EnableDynamicAgentLoading to hide this warning
WARNING: If a serviceability tool is not in use, please run
with -Djdk.instrument.traceUsage for more information
```

CHAPTER 4 WORKING WITH AUDIO

```
WARNING: Dynamic loading of agents will be disallowed by
default in a future release
Daisy, Daisy, give me your answer, too. I'm half crazy, all for
the love of you. It won't be a stylish marriage. I can't afford
a carriage. But you'd look sweet on the seat of a bicycle built
for two.
[INFO] Tests run: 1, Failures: 0, Errors: 0, Skipped: 0, Time
elapsed: 3.347 s -- in ch04.TranscribeTest
```

The neat thing to consider here is that the phrase is actually rendered pretty well; we expect it to render the *number* two (as in "a bicycle built for two") and not the homonym "too"—the AI model is usually going to infer the proper words based on the phrases in the song, so while the punctuation and capitalization may be slightly variable, *in general* it's rendering a quite recognizable transcription of the input, *without* necessarily recognizing the song itself.

The following table shows many of the transcription options available in this module of Spring AI and passed on to OpenAI.

Property	Description
spring.ai.openai.audio.transcription.options.model	ID of the model to use. Only whisper-1 (which is powered by our open source Whisper V2 model) is currently available.
spring.ai.openai.audio.transcription.options.response-format	The format of the transcript output, in one of these options: json, text, srt, verbose_json, or vtt.
spring.ai.openai.audio.transcription.options.prompt	An optional text to guide the model's style or continue a previous audio segment. The prompt should match the audio language.

(continued)

Property	Description
spring.ai.openai.audio. transcription.options.language	The language of the input audio. Supplying the input language in ISO-639-1 format will improve accuracy and latency.
spring.ai.openai.audio. transcription.options. temperature	The sampling temperature, between 0 and 1. Higher values like 0.8 will make the output more random, while lower values like 0.2 will make it more focused and deterministic. If set to 0, the model will use log probability to automatically increase the temperature until certain thresholds are hit.
spring.ai.openai.audio. transcription.options. timestamp_granularities	The timestamp granularities to populate for this transcription. response_format must be set verbose_json to use timestamp granularities. Either or both of these options are supported: word or segment. Note: There is no additional latency for segment timestamps, but generating word timestamps incurs additional latency.

REST Example

A real-world example might be an endpoint using Spring MVC which processes text or audio files. Our next step will be setting up two simple POST endpoints, one which accepts a String of text and the other which accepts an audio file.

Calling this endpoint might look something like this.

Listing 4-12. Calling the TTS endpoint with Daisy Bell lyrics

```
curl -X POST http://localhost:8080/api/tts \
-H "Content-Type: application/json" \
--output test.mp3 \
--data-binary @- << EOF
{"text": "Daisy, Daisy, \nGive me your answer, do! \nI'm half
crazy, \nAll for the love of you! \nIt won't be a stylish
marriage, \nI can't afford a carriage, \nBut you'll look sweet
upon the seat \nOf a bicycle built for two!"}
EOF
```

The above is passing a JSON object with a key of text and the value as the string we're looking to pass in. Running this command will look like the following depending on what text you pass in. For our case, we're passing in the contents of the song.

```
curl -X POST http://localhost:8080/api/tts \
-H "Content-Type: application/json" \
--output test.mp3 \
--data-binary @- << EOF
{"text": "Daisy, Daisy, \nGive me your answer, do! \nI'm half
crazy, \nAll for the love of you! \nIt won't be a stylish
marriage, \nI can't afford a carriage, \nBut you'll look sweet
upon the seat \nOf a bicycle built for two!"}
EOF
  % Total    % Received % Xferd  Average Speed   Time    Time     Time  Current
                                 Dload  Upload   Total   Spent    Left  Speed
100  240k  100  240k  100   229  97535     90  0:00:02  0:00:02 --:--:-- 97650
```

CHAPTER 4 WORKING WITH AUDIO

For transcribing an audio file containing spoken words, we can imagine the curl command to look like this.

Listing 4-13. Sending the Daisy Bell audio file to transcribe endpoint

```
curl -X POST http://localhost:8080/api/transcribe \
-F "file=@./src/test/resources/Daisy_Bell_sung_by_DECtalk.flac"
```

Running this from the chapter root should pick up the file that was downloaded earlier in the chapter and imagine it would return back the transcribed text. Output from this file will look something like the following:

```
% curl -X POST http://localhost:8080/api/transcribe \
-F "file=@./src/test/resources/Daisy_Bell_sung_by_DECtalk.flac"
Daisy, Daisy, give me your answer, do. I'm half-crazy all for
the love of you. It won't be a stylish marriage, I can't afford
a carriage. But you'd look sweet on the seat of a bicycle built
for two.
```

We'll start our implementation by creating a simple data class called `TextToSpeechRequest` which we can use for our endpoint `/api/tts`.

Listing 4-14. chapter04/src/main/java/ch04/model/TextToSpeechRequest.java

```
package ch04.model;

public record TextToSpeechRequest (String text) { }
```

After this our implementation will be fairly straightforward using Spring MVC. We will use dependency injection to insert our two services: `TextToSpeechService` and `TranscribeService`. Our two handlers will

115

CHAPTER 4   WORKING WITH AUDIO

accept POST requests with either a @RequestBody of TextToSpeechRequest as we saw above for processing the text to speech, or a `MultipartFile` for transcription.

Listing 4-15. chapter04/src/main/java/ch04/handler/ AudioTextController.java

```java
package ch04.handler;

import ch04.model.TextToSpeechRequest;
import ch04.service.TextToSpeechService;
import ch04.service.TranscribeService;
import ch04.service.VoiceAssistantService;
import org.springframework.core.io.ByteArrayResource;
import org.springframework.http.HttpHeaders;
import org.springframework.http.HttpStatus;
import org.springframework.http.ResponseEntity;
import org.springframework.web.bind.annotation.*;
import org.springframework.web.multipart.MultipartFile;
import org.springframework.web.server.ResponseStatusException;

import java.io.IOException;

@RestController
@RequestMapping("/api")
public class AudioTextController {

    private final TextToSpeechService textToSpeechService;

    private final TranscribeService transcribeService;

    private final VoiceAssistantService voiceAssistantService;

    public AudioTextController(TextToSpeechService textToSpeechService, TranscribeService transcribeService, VoiceAssistantService voiceAssistantService) {
```

CHAPTER 4 WORKING WITH AUDIO

```java
    this.textToSpeechService = textToSpeechService;
    this.transcribeService = transcribeService;
    this.voiceAssistantService = voiceAssistantService;
}

@PostMapping("/tts")
public ResponseEntity<byte> handleTextToSpeech(@RequestBody
TextToSpeechRequest textToSpeechRequest) {
    byte[] speechResult = textToSpeechService.
    processText(textToSpeechRequest.text(), null);

    HttpHeaders headers = new HttpHeaders();
    headers.add(HttpHeaders.CONTENT_DISPOSITION,
    "attachment; filename=output.mp3");
    headers.add(HttpHeaders.CONTENT_TYPE, "audio/mpeg");

    return new ResponseEntity(speechResult, headers,
    HttpStatus.OK);
}

@PostMapping("/transcribe")
public ResponseEntity<String> handleAudioUpload(@
RequestParam("file") MultipartFile file) {
    if (file.isEmpty()) {
        return new ResponseEntity<>("No file uploaded",
        HttpStatus.BAD_REQUEST);
    }

    try {
        var response = transcribeService.
        transcribeAudio(new ByteArrayResource(file.
        getBytes()), null);

        return new ResponseEntity<>(response.getResult().
```

```
getOutput(), HttpStatus.OK);
    } catch (IOException e) {
        return new ResponseEntity<>("Failed to upload
        file", HttpStatus.INTERNAL_SERVER_ERROR);
    }
}

@PostMapping("/assistant")
public ResponseEntity<byte[]> handleVoiceAssistantRequest
(@RequestParam("file") MultipartFile file) {
    if (file.isEmpty()) {
        throw new ResponseStatusException(HttpStatus.
        BAD_REQUEST, "No file uploaded");
    }

    try {
        var response = voiceAssistantService.issueCommand
        (new ByteArrayResource(file.getBytes()));

        return new ResponseEntity<>(response,
        HttpStatus.OK);
    } catch (IOException e) {
        throw new ResponseStatusException(HttpStatus.
        INTERNAL_SERVER_ERROR, "Failed to upload file");
    }
}
}
```

We can run this from the chapter root using Maven.

```
mvn -pl chapter04 -am spring-boot:run
```

CHAPTER 4   WORKING WITH AUDIO

After running spring-boot:run, you'll see output like below indicating that the server is running.

```
  .   ____          _            __ _ _
 /\\ / ___'_ __ _ _(_)_ __  __ _ \ \ \ \
( ( )\___ | '_ | '_| | '_ \/ _` | \ \ \ \
 \\/  ___)| |_)| | | | | || (_| |  ) ) ) )
  '  |____| .__|_| |_|_| |_\__, | / / / /
 =========|_|==============|___/=/_/_/_/
 :: Spring Boot ::                (v3.3.0)

2024-11-17T19:20:02.448-08:00  INFO 14015 --- [           main] ch04.Ch04Configuration                   : Starting Ch04Configuration using Java 21.0.3 with PID 14015 (/Users/kinabalu/workspace/beginningspring/bsai/code/chapter04/target/classes started by kinabalu in /Users/kinabalu/workspace/beginningspring/bsai/code/chapter04)
2024-11-17T19:20:02.449-08:00  INFO 14015 --- [           main] ch04.Ch04Configuration                   : No active profile set, falling back to 1 default profile: "default"
2024-11-17T19:20:02.864-08:00  INFO 14015 --- [           main] o.s.b.w.embedded.tomcat.TomcatWebServer  : Tomcat initialized with port 8080 (http)
2024-11-17T19:20:02.870-08:00  INFO 14015 --- [           main] o.apache.catalina.core.StandardService   : Starting service [Tomcat]
2024-11-17T19:20:02.870-08:00  INFO 14015 --- [           main] o.apache.catalina.core.StandardEngine    : Starting Servlet engine: [Apache Tomcat/10.1.24]
2024-11-17T19:20:02.895-08:00  INFO 14015 --- [           main] o.a.c.c.C.[Tomcat].[localhost].          : Initializing Spring embedded WebApplicationContext
```

```
2024-11-17T19:20:02.895-08:00  INFO 14015 --- [           main] 
w.s.c.ServletWebServerApplicationContext : Root 
WebApplicationContext: initialization completed in 365 ms 
2024-11-17T19:20:03.177-08:00  INFO 14015 --- [           main] 
o.s.b.w.embedded.tomcat.TomcatWebServer  : Tomcat started on 
port 8080 (http) with context path '/' 
2024-11-17T19:20:03.182-08:00  INFO 14015 --- [           main] 
ch04.Ch04Configuration                   : Started 
Ch04Configuration in 0.861 seconds (process running for 1.002) 
2024-11-17T19:20:37.051-08:00  INFO 14015 --- [nio-8080-exec-1] 
o.a.c.c.C.[Tomcat].[localhost].          : Initializing Spring 
DispatcherServlet 'dispatcherServlet' 
2024-11-17T19:20:37.051-08:00  INFO 14015 --- [nio-8080-exec-1] 
o.s.web.servlet.DispatcherServlet        : Initializing Servlet 
'dispatcherServlet' 
2024-11-17T19:20:37.052-08:00  INFO 14015 --- [nio-8080-
exec-1] o.s.web.servlet.DispatcherServlet        : Completed 
initialization in 1 ms
```

In a separate terminal session, we can use the curl commands above and see the API responses sent back similarly as with the tests.

A Simple Voice Assistant

Siri was the first voice-activated assistant available in a consumer device in early 2010. Likely due to it being the first and the compute power required it was mired in problems as it had to process speech using cloud servers and thus required a stable and fast Internet connection. Fast forward to today and thanks to the advancements in natural language processing and on-device hardware, we've moved to a context aware system that understands your speech and most requests you give it.

We are going to use what we've learned in this chapter and borrow code from the previous to create a simple virtual assistant. This is only a simple example, and if you were building an actual voice assistant, other choices would be more appropriate from a technology perspective.

The Voice Assistant Task

This task will create a new service called `VirtualAssistantService` which will make calls to the other two services we built in this chapter. In addition, we will add integration with the `UpdateChatService` from Chapter 3 to act on our lights via the chosen LLM.

We're going to take a slight shortcut for the audio command portion in our example and use the `TextToSpeechService` for creating the audio. If you would like to record the audio command yourself, we will call out how you can modify the `VoiceAssistantServiceTest` to pick up your file. If we think about this logically using the code we have today, we will be doing the following actions:

1. Generate the audio file with the command using the `TextToSpeechService`.

2. Take that audio file (or one you record yourself) and pass it to the `TranscribeService` to include in our prompt to `UpdateChatService`.

3. We'll pass the text from the `TranscribeService` to the `converse` method of `UpdateChatService` which calls the appropriate function based on the audio command.

4. Finally, we'll pass the text output of the `converse` method to the `TextToSpeechService` and save the resulting spoken word audio to disk.

CHAPTER 4 WORKING WITH AUDIO

With that, our first task is including Chapter 3 in our maven configuration files. This will let us re-use the services and methods involved in our ability to manage the real world we created in the previous chapter of light management using the LLM. We're including the updated `pom.xml` which includes a reference to `chapter03`.

Listing 4-16. chapter04/pom.xml

```xml
<?xml version="1.0" encoding="UTF-8"?>
<project xmlns="http://maven.apache.org/POM/4.0.0"
         xmlns:xsi="http://www.w3.org/2001/XMLSchema-instance"
         xsi:schemaLocation="http://maven.apache.org/POM/4.0.0
         http://maven.apache.org/xsd/maven-4.0.0.xsd">
    <modelVersion>4.0.0</modelVersion>
    <parent>
        <groupId>com.apress</groupId>
        <artifactId>bsai-code</artifactId>
        <version>1.0</version>
    </parent>

    <artifactId>chapter04</artifactId>
    <version>1.0</version>

    <properties>
    </properties>

    <dependencies>
        <dependency>
            <groupId>com.apress</groupId>
            <artifactId>chapter03</artifactId>
            <version>1.0</version>
        </dependency>
```

```xml
<dependency>
    <groupId>org.springframework.ai</groupId>
    <artifactId>spring-ai-openai-spring-boot-starter
    </artifactId>
</dependency>
<dependency>
    <groupId>org.springframework.boot</groupId>
    <artifactId>spring-boot-starter-web</artifactId>
</dependency>
<dependency>
    <groupId>org.springframework.boot</groupId>
    <artifactId>spring-boot-starter-test</artifactId>
    <scope>test</scope>
    <exclusions>
        <exclusion>
            <groupId>com.vaadin.external.google
            </groupId>
            <artifactId>android-json</artifactId>
        </exclusion>
    </exclusions>
</dependency>
</dependencies>
<build>
    <plugins>
        <plugin>
            <groupId>org.springframework.boot</groupId>
            <artifactId>spring-boot-maven-plugin
            </artifactId>
            <configuration>
                <skip>false</skip>
            </configuration>
```

```xml
            <executions>
                <execution>
                    <goals>
                        <goal>repackage</goal>
                    </goals>
                </execution>
            </executions>
        </plugin>
    </plugins>
  </build>
</project>
```

Our next task is to modify our @Configuration to include the UpdateChatService along with its dependencies. We are also creating some mocked light status that we can act on with our voice assistant. Here's an updated Ch04Configuration file with those new elements defined.

Listing 4-17. chapter04/src/main/java/ch04/Ch04Configuration.java

```java
package ch04;

import ch03.model.Light;
import ch03.service.UpdateChatService;
import ch03.service.UpdateLightStatusFunction;
import ch03.service.LightService;
import ch03.service.RequestLightStatusFunction;
import org.springframework.ai.chat.client.ChatClient;
import org.springframework.boot.SpringApplication;
import org.springframework.boot.autoconfigure.SpringBootApplication;
```

```java
import org.springframework.context.ApplicationContext;
import org.springframework.context.annotation.Bean;
import org.springframework.context.annotation.Description;

@SpringBootApplication
public class Ch04Configuration {
    @Bean
    Light getYellowLight() {
        return new Light("yellow", false);
    }

    @Bean
    Light getRedLight() {
        return new Light("red", true);
    }

    @Bean
    Light getGreenLight() {
        return new Light("green", false);
    }

    @Bean
    Light getBlueLight() {
        return new Light("blue", true);
    }

    @Bean
    LightService getLightService(ApplicationContext context) {
        return new LightService(context);
    }

    @Bean("RequestLightStatusService")
    @Description("Get light status")
    RequestLightStatusFunction getRequestLightStatusFunction
    (LightService lightService) {
```

CHAPTER 4   WORKING WITH AUDIO

```
        return new RequestLightStatusFunction(lightService);
    }

    @Bean("ChangeLightStatusService")
    @Description("Change a light's state")
    UpdateLightStatusFunction getChangeLightStatusFunction
    (LightService lightService) {
        return new UpdateLightStatusFunction(lightService);
    }

    @Bean
    UpdateChatService getLightUpdateChatService(ChatClient.
    Builder builder) {
        return new UpdateChatService(builder);
    }

    public static void main(String[] args) {
        SpringApplication.run(Ch04Configuration.class, args);
    }
}
```

Due to all the work we've done previously, this is all the configuration necessary to make a voice assistant like we've mapped out work. Our next step is to write up a test for what we want to ask. As we promised earlier, we'll show you some code inline that can be used if you want to record your own voice command. For reference, the configuration above has the light states as the following:

Light Name	Status
yellow	Off
red	On
Green	Off
Blue	On

Let's take a look at a test which will send a "voice" command to our LLM asking it to "Turn on yellow light" and gets an spoken word audio file back in response.

Listing 4-18. chapter04/src/test/java/ch04/ VoiceAssistantTest.java

package ch04;

import ch04.service.VoiceAssistantService;
import org.junit.jupiter.api.Test;
import org.springframework.beans.factory.annotation.Autowired;
import org.springframework.boot.test.context.SpringBootTest;
import org.springframework.core.io.ByteArrayResource;

import java.io.IOException;
import java.nio.file.Files;
import java.nio.file.Paths;

import static org.junit.jupiter.api.Assertions.assertNotNull;

@SpringBootTest(webEnvironment = SpringBootTest.WebEnvironment.MOCK)
public class VoiceAssistantTest {

    @Autowired
    VoiceAssistantService voiceAssistantService;

    @Test
    void runVoiceAssistantCommand() **throws** IOException {
        byte[] audioCommandAsBytes = Files.readAllBytes(Paths.get("./voice_assistant_command.mp3"));
        byte[] audioResponseBytes = voiceAssistantService.issueCommand(**new** ByteArrayResource(audioCommandAsBytes));

CHAPTER 4 WORKING WITH AUDIO

```
//          byte[] audioResponseBytes = voiceAssistantService.
            issueCommand("Turn on yellow light.");
        assertNotNull(audioResponseBytes);
        Files.write(Paths.get("./voice_assistant_response.
        mp3"), audioResponseBytes);
    }
}
```

The test we crafted involves calling the VoiceAssistantService with text of "Turn on yellow light." and receives a byte array which is the MP3 audio file of the LLM response. After receiving the byte array, we assert that it's not null and write the MP3 file to disk.

Now it's time to implement our somewhat convoluted VoiceAssistantService that our test calls to see this thing working.

Listing 4-19. chapter04/src/main/java/ch04/service/VoiceAssistantService.java

```java
package ch04.service;

import ch03.service.UpdateChatService;
import org.springframework.ai.audio.transcription.AudioTranscriptionResponse;
import org.springframework.ai.chat.messages.UserMessage;
import org.springframework.core.io.ByteArrayResource;
import org.springframework.core.io.Resource;
import org.springframework.stereotype.Service;

import java.util.List;

@Service
public class VoiceAssistantService {

    private final UpdateChatService updateChatService;
```

CHAPTER 4 WORKING WITH AUDIO

```java
    private final TranscribeService transcribeService;

    private final TextToSpeechService textToSpeechService;

    public VoiceAssistantService(UpdateChatService
    updateChatService, TranscribeService transcribeService,
    TextToSpeechService textToSpeechService) {
        this.updateChatService = updateChatService;
        this.transcribeService = transcribeService;
        this.textToSpeechService = textToSpeechService;
    }

    public byte[] issueCommand(Resource capturedAudio) {
        AudioTranscriptionResponse response = transcribe
        Service.transcribeAudio(capturedAudio, null);

        String output = response.getResult().getOutput();
        var updateResponse = updateChatService.converse(
                List.of(
                        new UserMessage(output)
                )
        );

        return textToSpeechService.processText(updateResponse.
        getFirst().getOutput().getContent(), null);
    }

    public byte[] issueCommand(String commandText) {
        var responseAsBytes = textToSpeechService.processText
        (commandText, null);

        return this.issueCommand(new ByteArrayResource
        (responseAsBytes));
    }
}
```

We've implemented two methods here for `issueCommand`. The primary method takes a `Resource` which we expect to include the recorded speech command "Turn on yellow light"; the other uses the `TextToSpeechService` in case you don't have a way of recording audio and passing it to the service. For our test as written, it uses the method accepting a String to simplify the example. The method transcribes the audio file with spoken words in it, passes it to the `UpdateChatService` for processing using the "real world," and then takes the LLM's text response and returns it as spoken word audio.

Let's re-run our tests for `chapter04`:

`mvn clean test -am -pl chapter04`

If all worked as expected, there should be an audio file saved on the filesystem named "voice_assistant_response.mp3", and playing it on your system, it will contain a message like "The yellow light has been turned on." We have included the maven output from our run for the `VoiceAssistantTest` class below.

```
[INFO] ---------------------------------------------------------
[INFO]  T E S T S
[INFO] ---------------------------------------------------------
[INFO] Running ch04.VoiceAssistantTest
INFO   org.springframework.test.context.support.
AnnotationConfigContextLoaderUtils -- Could not detect default
configuration classes for test class [ch04.VoiceAssistantTest]:
VoiceAssistantTest does not declare any static, non-private,
non-final, nested classes annotated with @Configuration.
INFO   org.springframework.boot.test.context.
SpringBootTestContextBootstrapper -- Found
@SpringBootConfiguration ch04.Ch04Configuration for test class
ch04.VoiceAssistantTest
```

```
INFO   ch03.service.UpdateLightStatusFunction -- Changing status
for light: Request[color=yellow, on=true]
[INFO] Tests run: 1, Failures: 0, Errors: 0, Skipped: 0, Time
elapsed: 3.998 s -- in ch04.VoiceAssistantTest
```

As we indicated earlier, if you want to record your own audio command, you can change the test to accommodate loading an MP3 file and sending that through the process. Simply load your MP3 file (here we assume voice_assistant_command.mp3 as a name) and pass that to the issueCommand method wrapped in a ByteArrayResource.

Something like the following.

```
byte[] audioCommandAsBytes = Files.readAllBytes(Paths.
get("./voice_assistant_command.mp3"));
byte[] audioResponseBytes = voiceAssistantService.
issueCommand(new ByteArrayResource(audioCommandAsBytes));
```

There you have it, a voice assistant that understands you.

Next Steps

In our next chapter, we're going to look at image generation with Spring AI and object identification in images using the multimodality API.

CHAPTER 5

Generating Images

Generating and Recognizing Images

The 1960s were an important time for the process of image recognition and generation similar to what we explored with audio in the previous chapter. Early image recognition using computer vision systems was focused on simple geometric shapes which evolved into techniques like edge detection and template matching. The complexity inherent in an image meant that these early techniques while impressive for their time were unable to deal with anything more than a very structured environment.

Over the years with advancements in usage of neural networks for learning-based approaches and later Support Vector Machines and other feature-based methods, object detection and classification had reached a well-defined commercial appeal especially with faster available hardware. Fast-forward to the last 25 years, the development of Convolutional Neural Networks (CNNs) and advanced GPU processing has exploded the capabilities of image recognition. The techniques utilized in most of the chat models available via Spring AI use some variant of transformers like Vision Transformers to perform their work.

As of this writing, the following offerings can perform image recognition via Spring AI:

- OpenAI (e.g., GPT-4 and GPT-4o models)
- Ollama (e.g., LlaVa, Baklava, Llama3.2 models)

CHAPTER 5   GENERATING IMAGES

- Vertex AI Gemini (e.g., gemini-1.5-pro-001, gemini-1.5-flash-001 models)

- Anthropic Claude 3

Image generation has experienced a similar trajectory and progression over the past 60 years. Early efforts in the 1960s laid the foundation, advancing through the 1980s and 1990s with innovations in 3D modeling, texturing, and realistic lighting using mathematically simulated scenes. The field took a significant leap forward in the last 20 years with the invention of Generative Adversarial Networks by Ian Goodfellow, which used two neural networks in tandem to create convincingly realistic images. More recently, the advent of text-to-image generation models, starting with early examples like DALL-E 1, marked another transformative phase. In 2022, diffusion models entered the commercial mainstream with notable releases such as DALL-E 2, Midjourney, and Stable Diffusion, delivering unprecedented realism and image quality.

As of this writing, the following are offered by Spring AI for image generation:

- OpenAI
- QianFan
- StabilityAI
- ZhiPuAI

First task we'll do is to create our directory structure for this chapter. This can be created in the "project directory" as in previous chapters with the following command, if you're running a POSIX shell like `bash` or `zsh`.

Listing 5-1. Creating the project directory structure in POSIX

```
mkdir -p src/{main,test}/{java,resources}
```

CHAPTER 5   GENERATING IMAGES

This is *this chapter's* project file, and thus it's in a directory *under* the top-level directory, called `chapter05`, and the file is named `pom.xml`. A few items to note here, just as in Chapter 4, we are going to include the `chapter03` module for a fun final challenge and a library extension for `ImageIO` found at `https://github.com/haraldk/TwelveMonkeys` which enables dealing with `webp` images.[1] We have included a simple class which can write these files to disk and convert them to PNG before doing so.

Listing 5-2. `chapter05/pom.xml`

```xml
<?xml version="1.0" encoding="UTF-8"?>

<project xmlns="http://maven.apache.org/POM/4.0.0"
         xmlns:xsi="http://www.w3.org/2001/XMLSchema-instance"
         xsi:schemaLocation="http://maven.apache.org/POM/4.0.0
         http://maven.apache.org/xsd/maven-4.0.0.xsd">
    <modelVersion>4.0.0</modelVersion>
    <parent>
        <groupId>com.apress</groupId>
        <artifactId>bsai-code</artifactId>
        <version>1.0</version>
    </parent>

    <artifactId>chapter05</artifactId>
    <version>1.0</version>

    <properties>
    </properties>

    <dependencies>
        <dependency>
            <groupId>com.apress</groupId>
```

---

[1] OpenAI renders and sends down `webp` images in their API.

```xml
            <artifactId>chapter03</artifactId>
            <version>1.0</version>
        </dependency>
        <dependency>
            <groupId>org.springframework.ai</groupId>
            <artifactId>spring-ai-openai-spring-boot-starter
            </artifactId>
        </dependency>
        <dependency>
            <groupId>com.twelvemonkeys.imageio</groupId>
            <artifactId>imageio-webp</artifactId>
            <version>3.12.0</version>
        </dependency>
        <dependency>
            <groupId>org.springframework.boot</groupId>
            <artifactId>spring-boot-starter-test</artifactId>
            <scope>test</scope>
            <exclusions>
                <exclusion>
                    <groupId>com.vaadin.external.google
                    </groupId>
                    <artifactId>android-json</artifactId>
                </exclusion>
            </exclusions>
        </dependency>
    </dependencies>
</project>
```

Our application configuration will be automatic just like we've shown in previous chapters. Your OpenAI API key will again be fed into the property `spring.ai.openai.api-key`. Our configuration will also include

CHAPTER 5   GENERATING IMAGES

getters for the yellow, red, green, and blue light properties, and setting up for the services and functions made available from the ch03 module to poll lights through ChatGPT and update their state.

Listing 5-3. chapter05/src/main/java/ch05/Ch05Configuration.java

```java
package ch05;

import ch03.model.Light;
import ch03.service.LightService;
import ch03.service.RequestLightStatusFunction;
import ch03.service.UpdateChatService;
import ch03.service.UpdateLightStatusFunction;
import org.springframework.ai.chat.client.ChatClient;

import org.springframework.boot.SpringApplication;
import org.springframework.boot.autoconfigure.SpringBootApplication;
import org.springframework.context.ApplicationContext;
import org.springframework.context.annotation.Bean;
import org.springframework.context.annotation.Configuration;
import org.springframework.context.annotation.Description;

@SpringBootApplication
@Configuration
public class Ch05Configuration {

    @Bean
    Light getYellowLight() {
        return new Light("yellow", false);
    }

    @Bean
    Light getRedLight() {
        return new Light("red", true);
    }
```

CHAPTER 5   GENERATING IMAGES

```
@Bean
Light getGreenLight() {
    return new Light("green", false);
}

@Bean
Light getBlueLight() {
    return new Light("blue", true);
}

@Bean
LightService getLightService(ApplicationContext context) {
    return new LightService(context);
}

@Bean("RequestLightStatusService")
@Description("Get light status")
RequestLightStatusFunction getRequestLightStatusFunction
(LightService lightService) {
    return new RequestLightStatusFunction(lightService);
}

@Bean("ChangeLightStatusService")
@Description("Change a light's state")
UpdateLightStatusFunction getChangeLightStatusFunction(Ligh
tService lightService) {
    return new UpdateLightStatusFunction(lightService);
}

@Bean
UpdateChatService getLightUpdateChatService(ChatClient.
Builder builder) {
    return new UpdateChatService(builder);
}
```

```
    public static void main(String[] args) {
        SpringApplication.run(Ch05Configuration.class, args);
    }
}
```

The OpenAiImageApi has a single request module OpenAiImageRequest which at a minimum would include the prompt we'd use for instructing either the generation which invokes DALL-E or the recognition which invokes CLIP. You will get a sense of the available options from the table below which can be included in properties or passed in with the request.

Property name	Description
spring.ai.openai.api-key	The API key to be used by the application. Again for some reason, this isn't utilized by OpenAiImageApi, but we'll continue with this convention here.
spring.ai.openai.organization-id	Optionally specify the organization to use in the API request.
spring.ai.openai.project-id	Optionally specify the project used for this API request.

The prefix spring.ai.openai.image is the property prefix that let's you configure the ImageModel implementation for OpenAI.

Property name	Description
spring.ai.openai.image.enabled	Enable OpenAI image model (we don't know why you would want to disable this but there you go).
spring.ai.opcnai.image.options.n	Images to generate, for dall-e-3 n=1 but can be up to 10 for dall-e-2.

(*continued*)

Property name	Description
spring.ai.openai.image.options.model	The model to use for image generation. The OpenAiImageApi.DEFAULT_IMAGE_MODEL is dall-e-3, but you can specify dall-e-2 as well for speed and cost.
spring.ai.openai.image.options.quality	Image quality by default will be standard, but if using the dall-e-3 model, you can specify hd, and the image will have finer details and greater consistency across the image.
spring.ai.openai.image.options.response_format	The format in which the generated images are returned. Must be one of URL or b64_json.
spring.ai.openai.image.options.size	Size of generated images. Must be one of 256x256, 512x512, or 1024x1024 for dall-e-2. Must be one of 1024x1024, 1792x1024, or 1024x1792 for dall-e-3 models.
spring.ai.openai.image.options.size_width	Width of the generated images. Must be one of 256, 512, or 1024 for dall-e-2.
spring.ai.openai.image.options.size_height	Height of the generated images. Must be one of 256, 512, or 1024 for dall-e-2.
spring.ai.openai.image.options.style	Style of the generated images. Either vivid or natural. Vivid causes the model to lean toward generating hyper-real and dramatic images. Natural causes the model to produce more natural, less hyper-real looking images. This parameter is only supported for dall-e-3.
spring.ai.openai.image.options.user	A unique identifier representing your end user, which can help OpenAI to monitor and detect abuse.

CHAPTER 5 GENERATING IMAGES

This chapter similar to Chapter 4 will include all tests which will perform executions against the OpenAI API. We will have the opportunity to go a bit deeper and use both the image generation and recognition pieces of the API in concert to create a silly but useful execution path utilizing Spring AI's image and multimodal modules.[2]

Image Generation

Our first test case will be a simple prompt for generating an image. It is incredible to think about the mountain of image data and technological achievement that is involved in taking a random set of text input and creating an image to represent it. At a super high level, the text that is entered is tokenized with a transformer and converted into a high-dimensional embedding. That embedding is then mapped to a shared latent space where the relationship between text and visual concepts is learned. The latent space is then passed through a generative diffusion model to create an image using the text embeddings and decoded into an image using CLIP contrastive learning model.

The text prompt we're using asks DALL-E to imagine a bowl of fruit containing bananas, apples, and kiwis. Our code calls the `ImageGeneratorService` which passes back a base64 encoded image included in a JSON object.

Listing 5-4. chapter05/src/test/java/ch05/GenerateImageTest.java

```
package ch05;

import ch05.service.ImageGeneratorService;
import org.junit.jupiter.api.Test;
import org.springframework.beans.factory.annotation.Autowired;
```

---

[2] Multimodal refers to the capability of processing or understanding multiple data modality types such as text, images, audio, and video.

CHAPTER 5   GENERATING IMAGES

```
import org.springframework.boot.test.context.SpringBootTest;

import javax.imageio.ImageIO;
import java.awt.image.BufferedImage;
import java.io.ByteArrayInputStream;
import java.io.IOException;
import java.util.Base64;

import static org.junit.jupiter.api.Assertions.assertNotNull;

@SpringBootTest
public class GenerateImageTest {

    @Autowired
    ImageGeneratorService imageGeneratorService;

    @Test
    void runImageGenerationQuery() {
        var image = imageGeneratorService.processPrompt(
                "Can you create an artistic rendering of a bowl
                full of fruit including only bananas, apples
                and kiwis",null
        );
        assertNotNull(image);

        byte[] binaryData = Base64.getDecoder().decode(image.getB64Json());
        try (ByteArrayInputStream webpStream = new ByteArrayInputStream(binaryData)) {
            BufferedImage bufferedImage = ImageIO.read(webpStream);
            assertNotNull(binaryData);
            WebpToPngConverter.convertWebpToPng(bufferedImage,
            "./rendered_fruit_bowl.png");
```

```
        } catch (IOException e) {
            System.err.println("IO Error while writing file:
            " + e.getMessage());
        }
    }
}
```

In a test first methodology we've now got something that will definitely not pass because it won't compile without an implementation of `ImageGeneratorService`. We'll get to the implementation of that in just a moment.

For now, the image that gets passed back, if you are interested in the output as part of the test the second half of the test writes the file to disk. OpenAI generated images are in webp format when they are sent down the wire. The webp format is currently the gold standard for web and mobile applications due to its more efficient file size and support in all modern browsers today. For saving and importing into a design tool though, we can't help but love png for this, so we've included a converter from webp to png.

Listing 5-5. chapter05/src/main/java/ch05/WebpToPngConverter.java

```
package ch05;

import javax.imageio.ImageIO;
import java.awt.image.BufferedImage;
import java.io.File;
import java.io.IOException;

public class WebpToPngConverter {

    public static void convertWebpToPng(BufferedImage webpImage, String pngPath) {
```

CHAPTER 5   GENERATING IMAGES

```
    try {
        ImageIO.write(webpImage, "png", new File(pngPath));

        System.out.println("Conversion complete: " +
        pngPath);
    } catch (IOException e) {
        System.err.println("Failed to convert WEBP to PNG:
        " + e.getMessage());
    }
  }
}
```

Now we get to the implementation of the `ImageGeneratorService` which has a singular and very simple method called `processPrompt(String, OpenAiImageOptions.Builder)` which takes a text prompt and an `OpenAiImageOptions` object which if null is passed we'll insert some defaults using the `application.properties` as specified.

With the text prompt given, we issue a call to the API we use `call()` to get the response back from the API which will interface with DALL-E and returns back the output of the `ImageResponse` returned.

Let's take a look at the actual class and what the implementation looks like.

Listing 5-6. chapter05/src/main/java/ch05/service/ImageGeneratorService.java

```
package ch05.service;

import org.springframework.ai.image.Image;
import org.springframework.ai.image.ImageOptionsBuilder;
import org.springframework.ai.image.ImagePrompt;
import org.springframework.ai.image.ImageResponse;
import org.springframework.ai.openai.OpenAiImageModel;
```

CHAPTER 5   GENERATING IMAGES

```java
import org.springframework.ai.openai.OpenAiImageOptions;
import org.springframework.stereotype.Service;

@Service
public class ImageGeneratorService {

    private final OpenAiImageModel openAiImageModel;

    public ImageGeneratorService(OpenAiImageModel
    openAiImageModel) {
        this.openAiImageModel = openAiImageModel;
    }

    public Image processPrompt(String prompt, OpenAiImage
    Options.Builder imageOptions) {
        var imagePrompt = imageOptions != null ? new
        ImagePrompt(prompt, imageOptions.build()) : new
        ImagePrompt(prompt,
                ImageOptionsBuilder.builder().withWidth(1024).
                withHeight(1024).build());
        ImageResponse response = openAiImageModel.call
        (imagePrompt);
        return response.getResult().getOutput();
    }
}
```

Let's generate an image since our test will pass. We'll call the chapter's test suite using Maven:

```
mvn -am -pl chapter05 clean test
```

CHAPTER 5   GENERATING IMAGES

The image that gets output will save in the top-level directory of our system. After our prompt, the following was what DALL-E generated for us.[3]

Our generative fruit bowl

If everything is working properly, it should complete with SUCCESS. After a successful run, you can check the root of the projects filesystem and should see a new png image named rendered_fruit_bowl.png which will contain an image representation of what DALL-E thinks a fruit bowl looks like with bananas, apples, and kiwis.

---

[3] Readers might notice that our image has a friend, isn't he cute?

Multimodality Recognition

Now that we have an image that we have generated, we can use this in a test of the multimodality integration. Our test will take a generated image from DALL-E, and we can query and ask questions about it in the "text" mode. We'll again lean on using OpenAI as the source for our artificial intelligence needs, and we can recycle the fruit bowl we just generated for our next test.

Our test will consist of two items that we'll be passing to the API: a prompt and an image. For the image, we'll load it using a `FileSystemResource` and pulling from the top-level directory.

We'll take the `Resource` and the text prompt. `In a single sentence explain what is in this picture and identify every item`, and at the end, do some simple assertions to ensure that the text description contains the words "banana," "apple," and "kiwi."

Listing 5-7. chapter05/src/test/java/ch05/ImageRecognitionTest.java

```java
package ch05;

import ch05.service.ImageRecognitionService;
import org.junit.jupiter.api.Test;
import org.springframework.ai.model.Media;
import org.springframework.beans.factory.annotation.Autowired;
import org.springframework.boot.test.context.SpringBootTest;
import org.springframework.core.io.ClassPathResource;
import org.springframework.core.io.FileSystemResource;
import org.springframework.util.MimeTypeUtils;

import static org.junit.jupiter.api.Assertions.assertTrue;

@SpringBootTest
public class ImageRecognitionTest {
```

```
    @Autowired
    ImageRecognitionService imageRecognitionService;

    @Test
    void runImageRecognitionQuery() {
        var imageResource = new FileSystemResource("rendered_
        fruit_bowl.png");
        Media renderedFruitBowl = new Media(MimeTypeUtils.
        IMAGE_PNG, imageResource);
        String recognition = imageRecognitionService.identify(
                "In a single sentence explain what is in this
                picture and identify every item.",
                renderedFruitBowl);

        System.out.println(recognition);
        assertTrue(recognition.contains("banana"));
        assertTrue(recognition.contains("apple"));
        assertTrue(recognition.contains("kiwi"));
    }
}
```

One thing you'll notice is we are outputting the contents of the recognition object returned to stdout. We've left this in because during the testing of this book, the hallucinations sometimes cause a test to fail, and it helps to see why the assertions fail.

The other thing you'll see is that we can't quite run this yet since the ImageRecognitionService doesn't exist. Let's take a look at the implementation of ImageRecognitionService and see how the multimodality integration of interrogating an image via a prompt is done.

Listing 5-8. chapter05/src/main/java/ch05/service/ImageRecognitionService.java

```java
package ch05.service;

import org.springframework.ai.chat.messages.UserMessage;
import org.springframework.ai.chat.model.ChatModel;
import org.springframework.ai.chat.model.ChatResponse;
import org.springframework.ai.chat.prompt.Prompt;
import org.springframework.ai.model.Media;
import org.springframework.stereotype.Service;

@Service
public class ImageRecognitionService {

    private final ChatModel chatModel;

    public ImageRecognitionService(ChatModel chatModel) {
        this.chatModel = chatModel;
    }

    public String identify(String prompt, Media media) {
        var userMessage = new UserMessage(
                prompt,
                media);

        ChatResponse response = chatModel.call(new Prompt(userMessage));

        return response.getResult().getOutput().getContent();
    }
}
```

We have a `ChatModel` available in this class which we'll use Spring's dependency injection to reference in our `ImageRecognitionService`.

CHAPTER 5   GENERATING IMAGES

Our call to OpenAI is building a `UserMessage` which will contain the two items passed in via the test: a text prompt and the Media object. Our call to the API will be blocking, so we'll use `call()` to get the response specification.

With our response, we can pass back the description from OpenAI on what is inside the image. For our usage and this test, we don't need the metadata, but just know that it's available if needed for your application.

Now that we have a service, our tests should pass. We'll call the chapter's test suite using Maven:

```
mvn -am -pl chapter05 clean test
```

If mercury isn't in retrograde in the OpenAI cloud, you should see SUCCESS in the test. The test itself will print out the returned text from OpenAI, and the test itself should also pass. We have deliberately written a test that depends on the generation from a previously written test `GenerateImageTest` which is not a best practice so in the future best to avoid dependencies.

We've included a test run so you can see it working end to end.

```
[INFO] -------------------------------------------------------
[INFO]  T E S T S
[INFO] -------------------------------------------------------
[INFO] Running ch05.ImageRecognitionTest
12:26:03.366 [main] INFO org.springframework.test.context.
support.AnnotationConfigContextLoaderUtils -- Could not
detect default configuration classes for test class [ch05.
ImageRecognitionTest]: ImageRecognitionTest does not declare
any static, non-private, non-final, nested classes annotated
with @Configuration.
12:26:03.405 [main] INFO org.springframework.boot.test.context
.SpringBootTestContextBootstrapper -- Found @SpringBoot
Configuration ch05.Ch05Configuration for test class ch05.
ImageRecognitionTest
```

CHAPTER 5 GENERATING IMAGES

```
Powered by Spring Boot 3.3.0
2024-11-16T12:26:03.548-08:00  INFO 79859 --- [           main]
ch05.ImageRecognitionTest              : Starting
ImageRecognitionTest using Java 21.0.3 with PID 79859 (started
by kinabalu in /Users/kinabalu/workspace/beginningspring/bsai/
code/chapter05)
2024-11-16T12:26:03.550-08:00  INFO 79859 --- [           main]
ch05.ImageRecognitionTest              : No active profile
set, falling back to 1 default profile: "default"
2024-11-16T12:26:04.248-08:00  INFO 79859 --- [           main]
ch05.ImageRecognitionTest              : Started
ImageRecognitionTest in 0.798 seconds (process running
for 1.173)
WARNING: A Java agent has been loaded dynamically (/Users/
kinabalu/.m2/repository/net/bytebuddy/byte-buddy-agent/1.14.16/
byte-buddy-agent-1.14.16.jar)
WARNING: If a serviceability tool is in use, please run
with -XX:+EnableDynamicAgentLoading to hide this warning
WARNING: If a serviceability tool is not in use, please run
with -Djdk.instrument.traceUsage for more information
WARNING: Dynamic loading of agents will be disallowed by
default in a future release
The image shows a bowl containing a red apple, a yellow apple,
and two bananas, with sliced kiwis and kiwi seeds on a wooden
surface.
[INFO] Tests run: 1, Failures: 0, Errors: 0, Skipped: 0, Time
elapsed: 5.366 s -- in ch05.ImageRecognitionTest
[INFO] Running ch05.GenerateImageTest
2024-11-16T12:26:08.665-08:00  INFO 79859 --- [           main]
t.c.s.AnnotationConfigContextLoaderUtils : Could not
detect default configuration classes for test class [ch05.
GenerateImageTest]: GenerateImageTest does not declare any
```

151

CHAPTER 5 GENERATING IMAGES

static, non-private, non-final, nested classes annotated with
@Configuration.
2024-11-16T12:26:08.665-08:00 INFO 79859 --- [main]
.b.t.c.SpringBootTestContextBootstrapper : Found
@SpringBootConfiguration ch05.Ch05Configuration for test class
ch05.GenerateImageTest
Conversion complete: ./rendered_fruit_bowl.png
[INFO] Tests run: 1, Failures: 0, Errors: 0, Skipped: 0,
Time elapsed: 12.88 s -- in ch05.GenerateImageTest
[INFO]
[INFO] Results:
[INFO]
[INFO] Tests run: 2, Failures: 0, Errors: 0, Skipped: 0
[INFO]
[INFO] --
[INFO] Reactor Summary for bsai-code 1.0:
[INFO]
[INFO] bsai-code .... SUCCESS [0.140 s]
[INFO] chapter03 .... SUCCESS [12.635 s]
[INFO] chapter05 .... SUCCESS [19.162 s]
[INFO] --
[INFO] BUILD SUCCESS
[INFO] --
[INFO] Total time: 32.062 s
[INFO] Finished at: 2024-11-16T12:26:21-08:00
[INFO] --

One fun exercise you can try on your own is to expand your prompt to get more information about the media you upload to the API. We could imagine that uploading a PDF and asking it to summarize the contents could be another test of the multimodal nature of this module in Spring AI.

CHAPTER 5 GENERATING IMAGES

Lights, Camera, AI

For the last test, we're going to re-use the code from the lights in Chapter 3, and we're going to generate some images based on the lights' properties we've defined in `Ch05Configuration` which we're letting OpenAI use as a data source.

Here's the process for what the following test actually does, and the great part about it is we're not doing anything new here so as soon as we explain ourselves here we can run the test right away.

We've got three lights that are possible in our system and in the following test:

1. Ask the AI to create a prompt for DALL-E to generate an image of any lightbulb which is on.

2. Pass that prompt to the `ImageGeneratorService` and retrieve the `Image`.

3. Pass that `Image` back to the AI and ask it to explain what's in the picture.

4. Assert that at a minimum the explanation contains the word `red` since that's the light that should be turned on.

5. Run a command with OpenAI to turn off the red light, and turn on the green light.

6. Re-run steps 1–3 above again.

7. Assert that at a minimum the explanation contains the word `green` now since we turned off the red light and turned on the green in our command.

153

CHAPTER 5   GENERATING IMAGES

Let's take a look at how this works in the test below.

Listing 5-9.   chapter05/src/test/java/ch05/LightVisualizerTest.java

package ch05;

import ch03.service.UpdateChatService;
import ch05.service.ImageGeneratorService;
import ch05.service.ImageRecognitionService;
import org.junit.jupiter.api.Test;
import org.springframework.ai.chat.messages.UserMessage;
import org.springframework.ai.model.Media;
import org.springframework.beans.factory.annotation.Autowired;
import org.springframework.boot.test.context.SpringBootTest;
import org.springframework.ai.image.Image;

import org.springframework.core.io.ByteArrayResource;
import org.springframework.util.MimeType;

import java.io.IOException;
import java.util.Base64;
import java.util.List;

import static org.junit.jupiter.api.Assertions.assertTrue;

@SpringBootTest
public class LightVisualizerTest {
    @Autowired
    ImageGeneratorService generatorService;

    @Autowired
    ImageRecognitionService recognitionService;

    @Autowired
    private UpdateChatService updateChatService;

154

CHAPTER 5   GENERATING IMAGES

```java
public static final MimeType IMAGE_WEBP = new
MimeType("image", "webp");

String runCommand(String prompt) {
    var updateResponse = updateChatService.converse(
            List.of(
                    new UserMessage(prompt)
            )
    );

    return updateResponse.getFirst().getOutput().
    getContent();
}

Media imageToMedia(Image image) throws IOException {
    byte[] binaryData = Base64.getDecoder().decode(image.
    getB64Json());
    return new Media(IMAGE_WEBP, new ByteArrayResource
    (binaryData));
}

@Test
void runLightVisualizer() {
    try {
        var initialLightbulbPrompt = runCommand("Based on
        the status of the lights red, yellow and green
        create a single sentence prompt for DALL-E of an
        realistic rendering of a lightbulb for any color
        which is turned on");
        var image = generatorService.processPrompt(
                initialLightbulbPrompt,null
        );
```

155

CHAPTER 5   GENERATING IMAGES

```
Media firstLightbulbMedia = imageToMedia(image);
String recognition = recognitionService.identify(
        "In a single sentence explain what is in
        this picture?",
        firstLightbulbMedia);

System.out.println(recognition);
assertTrue(recognition.toLowerCase().
contains("red"));

runCommand("Turn off red light and turn on green
light");

var newLightBulbRenderPrompt = runCommand("Based
on the status of the lights red, yellow and green
create a single sentence prompt for DALL-E of an
realistic rendering of a lightbulb for any color
which is turned on");

var newLightBulbImage = generatorService.
processPrompt(
        newLightBulbRenderPrompt,null
);

Media secondLightbulbMedia = imageToMedia(newLight
BulbImage);
String newRecognition = recognitionService.
identify(
        "In a single sentence explain what is in
        this picture?",
        secondLightbulbMedia);
System.out.println(newRecognition);
assertTrue(newRecognition.toLowerCase().
contains("green"));
```

```
        } catch (IOException e) {
            System.err.println("IO Error while writing file:
            " + e.getMessage());
        }
    }
}
```

Now that we have the test and it reuses existing services, we'll again call the chapter's test suite using Maven:

```
mvn -am -pl chapter05 clean test
```

Whew. We've got a test now performing the functions, and it should pass. One could imagine if you hooked up a camera that captured an image at some regular frequency and uploaded that capture to an AI, you could ask it to perform a function based on what it saw in the photo. Pretty neat.

Next Steps

In our next chapter, we'll wrap up with a discussion on navigating AI in engineering, the challenges, and share some best practices.

CHAPTER 6

Navigating AI in Engineering

Challenges and Best Practices

A Practical Exploration of AI-Aided Development

In Chapter 1, we brought up a simple high-level overview of the AI landscape as it is today. It's a useful chapter, not just because of the content it holds but because of the way it was written.

It was drafted in Asciidoctor[1] (as was the rest of the book), with the editor suggesting minor grammar changes as it was written. These edits were focused on simple things like matching tenses or spelling.[2]

---

[1] Asciidoctor (https://asciidoctor.org) is software for taking simple text content and generating a document model from it.

[2] If you're interested, the tool used for grammar and syntax was Grammarly, at https://grammarly.com/, which is merely one of many such tools, and this is not an endorsement of Grammarly over other similar tools like ProWritingAid (https://prowritingaid.com/), and so forth. Most of them do the same sorts of things, although most of them *also* tend to be more focused on specific types of writing; ProWritingAid, for example, is primarily meant for storytellers. Even Microsoft Word has similar grammar aids, like CoPilot.

CHAPTER 6　NAVIGATING AI IN ENGINEERING

After the initial simple draft was done and revised by the author, the content was submitted as a whole to an LLM (ChatGPT, specifically), with a prompt asking for hints toward readability, ease of use, and appropriate topical coverage. ChatGPT then presented a potential rewrite of the chapter, which wasn't quite what was intended.

That rewritten draft was then considered sentence-by-sentence and compared to the original. In some cases, the rewrite was indeed more clear, or highlighted issues in the original draft, and those changes were integrated into the chapter's content. The changes were not copied or accepted wholesale. Any original content suggested by ChatGPT was carefully considered before inclusion.

Only one section included new content suggested by ChatGPT, which was then rewritten before being added to the draft. Apart from the quote from ChatGPT (on the "summary of AI"), no content was quoted from ChatGPT as original material.

The other chapters also utilized similar aids. Grammar checkers were used throughout the writing process, and their suggestions were often accepted. Additionally, the text was submitted to the LLM for evaluation to improve clarity and completeness. The code, too, was evaluated by an LLM for suggestions for refactoring and efficiency, with some suggestions accepted and others rejected.

This text was written by humans, aided by AI, and not the other way around.[3]

---

[3] Of course, "written by humans and aided by AI, and not the other way around" is exactly what an AI author would be instructed to say, wouldn't it? The main proof we have that humans wrote this is in the revision history of the text, which includes some amusing and very human errors, and the silliness of some of the footnotes, which the AIs kept telling us to remove.

While this is a *book* and not a *program*, similar practices are emerging in programming. AI suggests revisions to code, deriving intent from the programmer and the code they write based on code structure, name choices, and the like. It can generate code based on prompts provided by the engineer, and it's up to the engineer to decide what to do with that code.

This is not without its dangers.

Dangers in Applying AI in Engineering

If there's a concern around AI, it's not about a possible future in which an AI overthrows humanity: it's in how easy it is to mistake AI-generated content as being accurate. Generating content with AI is easy and becoming easier all the time, and the AIs are getting better and better at generating realistic output, no matter what kind of medium is being used.

AI models depend heavily on the quality and suitability of their training data and are highly sensitive to data quality issues: "garbage in, garbage out" is very apt, and given the volume of data used to train even the smaller LLMs, it's very difficult to ensure that the data is correct; thus, it's relatively easy for an AI to confidently assert something that is very, very wrong.

AIs can generate working code relatively easily, and there are many AI models designed specifically for this purpose; asking an AI how to write a function to parse a given set of inputs, yielding a specific type of output, is likely to give you working code for whichever language you choose, and you can often even specify the parsing techniques.

CHAPTER 6 NAVIGATING AI IN ENGINEERING

For example, you could ask for the use of a packrat-style parser[4] in Java, with examples of seven input lines, and show the data you want to extract. Many of the AI models will generate full working code, including tests and suggestions of libraries.

The code will probably[5] even work. The danger here is that the AI will work *to your specification*, flaws and all, which means that the prompt needs to be as precise as possible, and even then, the generated code needs to be parsed carefully to make sure it **actually does what it's supposed to**. It might be reliable, but you need to verify that.

You're not getting rid of the need for a competent engineer just because an AI can generate code. Most experienced programmers can easily recount examples where a stakeholder described a complex process as "just process the order, it's obvious," only to find a complex problem lurking behind a simple request.

In the end, an AI is going to rely heavily on two things: your skill at specifying a problem clearly and precisely and your ability to evaluate whether the solution is appropriate.

There's no shortcut here.

Human expertise and critical thinking remain essential in effectively utilizing AI tools, although as the tools improve, they can help even when it comes to evaluating themselves.

---

[4] A "packrat-style parser" is a context-free parser. They tend to be quite fast, often very flexible, and their grammars can be a pain to write. See https://en.wikipedia.org/wiki/Parsing_expression_grammar for more details.

[5] Saying code will "probably" work should be offensive to competent programmers. Good programmers *know* whether their code works. That's part of why this book was written to be test-heavy.

Legal and Ethical Issues

AI also creates some interesting legal and ethical concerns. Since AI creates content modeled on others' work, there's a danger of it being too similar to the original, potentially infringing on copyright laws. This is without even considering the ethical implications of imitating someone else's work product.

For example, actors have filed lawsuits against some AI models' owners, claiming that their voices have been used by the AIs, without their permission. We could theoretically—but not necessarily legally or ethically—have an AI replicate a famous actor's voice in a production, with no credit or compensation offered to that actor.

What's more, there are significant concerns that extend beyond copyright law. There is a very real risk that AI could be misused to generate content that falsely represents real people, potentially damaging reputations, or spreading misinformation, or creating something that crosses the line from imitation into forgery.

Many of the models have been trained to attempt to avoid such violations; asking ChatGPT to create a painting in the style of Jackson Pollock, for example, creates a response that the image cannot be created due to content policy guidelines due to how uniquely identifiable Pollock's style is. (Each model has its own policies here; ChatGPT is being used as an example only.)

With that said, developers have trained models without these ethical and legal guardrails: users should exercise caution and ethical consideration when employing these models. They're not without purpose, but they should be approached with care.

If there are concerns about the legality of AI-generated content, it is advisable to consult a legal professional.

CHAPTER 6   NAVIGATING AI IN ENGINEERING

Data Visibility and Transparency

While the previous section discussed the legality of data produced by AI, it's also important to consider the legal and privacy implications of the data you provide to an AI hosted by a third party.[6]

When using a third-party service like ChatGPT, as we do throughout this book, you're sending information outside of your direct control. If your data is meant to be secure, submitting it to an external service can **violate** that security, because *you don't know what the service is doing with it*, a concern that goes beyond AI services, because you don't necessarily know what the services are doing with your data.

The service might log your data, and if those logs are hacked or exposed, your information could become compromised.

The service might use your contributed data to train future versions of its models, especially if it's operated by a social media conglomerate. This means your private data could become accessible to anyone who formulates the right prompt to extract it.

The services themselves have a strong interest in preventing these scenarios, of course; it's unlikely that *any* of the services are particularly interested in private or secured information in and of itself. Most of them, if not all of them, will have documentation around their security and training practices, and this documentation should be read carefully. Ultimately, it's up to users to ensure they understand the risks and take appropriate measures to safeguard their information.

---

[6] Local models offered by platforms like Ollama can offer enhanced data security compared to external services since they keep data on-premises. These models still should be checked to make sure they don't send information offsite, or isolated by firewalls to prevent possible breaches of security, but local models are **probably** safer than external services. They also require significant computational resources and can be slower or less efficient than cloud-based services. In any event, it's crucial for users to verify that even local models do not transmit data externally and to implement appropriate security measures to safeguard information.

> **Note** Depending on your locale, there may also be laws in place to govern what data you can send to external services, including but not limited to GDPR,[7] CCPA,[8] or HIPAA.[9] Please do not violate any laws.

The rule of thumb might be: **If someone can use this data to identify the subject of the prompt, it might be too private to send to an AI.** However, this is a *generalized rule* and shouldn't be taken as legal advice.

As with other legal and ethical concerns, a legal professional should be consulted if there's a question of whether data can be sent to an AI or not.

In summary, being mindful of the data you share with AI services is crucial to maintaining security and compliance with legal and ethical standards.

Effective Prompt Engineering

While this book does not delve into the intricacies of prompt engineering—doing so would likely double its length—it is important to acknowledge that prompts can create responses that are biased or harmful, and it's our responsibility as users of AI to be aware of potential biases and address such concerns accordingly.

---

[7] The text of the General Data Protection Regulation (GPDR) can be found at https://gdpr-info.eu/ and addresses the right and ownership of individual data in the European Union.

[8] CCPA is the California Consumer Privacy Act, found at https://www.oag.ca.gov/privacy/ccpa, and can be considered sort of an analog to the GDPR.

[9] The Health Insurance Portability and Accountability Act (HIPAA) can be found at https://www.hhs.gov/hipaa/index.html and addresses patients' rights to privacy in the United States.

To illustrate this point without delving into extensive detail, prompt writers should be aware of how prompts can change the responses, by embedding assumptions.

Assumptions in prompts might be entirely benign or innocuous: "Describe a teacher who loves her students," for example, *presumes* that the teacher is female as part of the question. While this may be intentional—for instance, if focusing on a female teacher—it might also be an unintentional bias. A better query *might* be "Describe a teacher who loves their students," using gender-neutral language, unless gender is *intended* to be part of the response.

Even if a neutral question is asked, the response might be biased. A prompt asking for a description of a successful entrepreneur might get a consistent description of a male, for example, even though there are certainly successful female entrepreneurs.

These biases occur because AI models are trained on existing data, which may reflect societal biases. As a result, the AI might be more likely to produce responses that align with those biases. If the models have more references to male business leaders than female entrepreneurs, then the models will themselves more likely describe entrepreneurs as male.

This reinforcement means that the common knowledge pool—which future models may use for training—contains even more references to successful male entrepreneurs. This creates a feedback loop, amplifying the bias without any malicious intent.

Models being trained on common knowledge also have to wrestle with the possibility that common knowledge is *wrong*. An engineer had a rather appropriate observation on LinkedIn:

> *I'm going to be very wary of large-language models and AI in general until I find one that can say, "I don't know," when I ask a question about a technical matter. Generally, they behave like really eager interns that would rather make up an answer than admit to not knowing the answer.*
>
> —Paul Parks, https://www.linkedin.com/posts/paulmooreparks_ai-llm-activity-7240264719364673536-GpFJ

Therefore, it's crucial for anyone interacting with AI systems to continually remain vigilant about these biases and actively work to mitigate them in pursuit of accuracy, honesty, and integrity.

Next Steps

We've reached the end of the journey for *this* particular book.

We've tried to focus on those elements from Spring AI that would prove most useful for most programmers, while acknowledging that there are a lot of use cases that go deeper in nearly everything we've touched.

Such is the nature of an introductory book. We'd like to invite you to explore and create using the technology, going as far as your imagination and skills can take you, and we wish you success in all that you do; show us what you've done, and tell us what we can do better!

Thank you.

Index

A, B

AI, *see* Artificial intelligence (AI)
API, *see* Application programming interface (API)
Application programming interface (API), 25
Artificial intelligence (AI)
  approaches, 3
  assumptions, 166
  content generation, 161
  costs/high-quality/large model, 10, 11
  data quality issues, 161
  data/reasoning process, 57–59
  definition, 1, 3
  external service, 164
  features, 1
  Grammar checkers, 160
  information blenders, 7
  legal and ethical concerns, 163
  LLMs (*see* Large Language Models (LLMs))
  Markov chain, 4, 6
  matching tenses/spelling, 159
  mathematical models, 3
  prompt engineering, 165–167
  rewritten draft, 160
  services, 8, 9, 164, 165
Asciidoctor, 159
Audio process/generation
  AudioTextController, 116
  definition, 95
  integrations, 96
  real-world application, 113–120
  text-to-speech (*see* Text-to-speech technology)
  TextToSpeechRequest, 115
  transcription
    FLAC file, 107
    properties, 112, 113
    response specification, 110
    testing process, 107–112
    TranscribeService, 109, 110
  voice assistant
    configuration, 126, 127
    definition, 120
    configuration, 124–126
    pom.xml file, 122–124
    task process, 121–131
    VoiceAssistant Service, 128–130
    VoiceAssistantTest class, 127, 128, 130, 131

INDEX

C

ChatGPT, 3, 12
CNNs, *see* Convolutional Neural Networks (CNNs)
Convolutional Neural Networks (CNNs), 133

D, E, F, G, H

Data structure, 57
    human interaction, 93
    providing access, 71
        apply() method, 80
        buildOptions() method, 90
        content summary, 72
        converse() method, 90
        entity() method, 88
        light information, 81–87
        RequestChatService, 75–77
        RequestLightStatus Function, 78, 79
        RequestLightStatusTest, 74, 75, 80
        Spring configuration, 72
        structured output, 87–92
        UpdateChatService, 83
        UpdateLightStatus Function, 81
        UpdateLightStatusTest, 85
        UpdateLight StructuredTest, 90
    real world application, 59–71
Different models, 33–36

I

Image recognition/generation application
    configuration, 136–139
    computer vision systems, 133
    concepts, 133
    DALL-E generation, 146, 147
    diffusion models, 134
    feature-based methods, 133
    GenerateImageTest, 141–143
    ImageGenerator Service, 144, 145
    lights/camera, 153–157
    multimodality integration, 147–152
    OpenAiImageApi, 139–141
    pom.xml file, 135, 136
    POSIX shell, 134
    properties, 139
    text and visual concepts, 141
    WebpToPngConverter, 143, 144

J, K

Java, Maven project structure, 13–22
Java programming, 11

L

Large Language Models (LLMs), 3
    definition, 6
    current events, 58

LinkedIn, 166
LLMs, *see* Large Language
    Models (LLMs)

M, N

Maven project, 11
    audio process/generation, 118
    project structure, 13–22
    text-to-speech
        technology, 104

O

OpenAI
    access key, 21
    API settings page, 26
    application.properties, 28
    ChatClient, 27, 28
    configuration, 26
    env file, 26
    FirstChatService
        implementation, 31, 32
    keys, 25
    lightbulbs, 59–61
    project creation, 24
    response
        specification, 29, 30
    screenshot, 32
    settings, 25
    settings screen, 23
    spring-boot-starter-web, 18–20
openHAB, 59

P, Q, R

Project structure
    bsai-code, 14
    .env file, 21, 22
    Maven directory structure, 14
    OpenAI, 18–20
    pom.xml, 14–18
    POSIX creation, 14

S

Smart lightbulbs
    BaseLightTests class, 67–69
    directory structure, 60
    getBeansOfType() method, 65
    getLights(), 65
    light class, 62, 63
    LightService, 69–71
    configuration class, 66–68
    pom.xml, 60–62
    services, 63–65
Spring framework AI, *see* Artificial
        intelligence (AI)
    abstraction, 22
    audio (*see* Audio process/
        generation)
    chat models, 22
    coarse abstractions, 22
    conversation/roles, 48
        ConversationTests, 50–53
        interactiveConversation()
            method, 53

Spring framework AI (*cont.*)
    Prompt object, 48
    system message, 55
    UpdateChatService, 49, 50
    UserMessage, 54, 55
  different models, 33–36
  image (*see* Image recognition/
    generation)
  lightbulbs (*see* Smart
    lightbulbs)
  OpenAI, 22–26
  temperature
    differences, 43, 44
    JaccardSimilarity
     Calculator, 39–41
    n-grams, 38, 43
    OpenAiChatOptions, 37
    probability mass, 37
    testing code, 41, 42
    VariabilityTests, 44–47

T, U, V, W, X, Y, Z

Text-to-speech technology
  application
    configuration, 99, 100
  history, 96
  OpenAiAudioSpeech
    Options, 105–107
  pom.xml file, 97–99
  project directory structure, 97
  properties, 100
  SpeechTTSTest, 101, 102
  TextToSpeechService, 103, 104

The manufacturer's authorised representative in the EU is Springer Nature Customer Service Centre GmbH, Europaplatz 3, 69115 Heidelberg, Germany. If you have any concerns regarding our products, please contact ProductSafety@springernature.com

Printed and bound by CPI Group (UK) Ltd, Croydon, CR0 4YY

26/03/2026

02078971-0001